MTLE Minnesota Special Education Core Skills (Birth to Age 21)

Teacher Certification Exam

By: Sharon Wynne, M.S.

XAMonline, INC.

Boston

To obtain permission(s) to use the material from this work for any purpose including workshops or seminars, please submit a written request to:

XAMonline, Inc.
25 First Street, Suite 106
Cambridge, MA 02141
Toll Free: 1-800-509-4128
Email: info@xamonline.com
Web: www.xamonline.com
Fax: 1-617-583-5552

Library of Congress Cataloging-in-Publication Data

Wynne, Sharon A.
   Minnesota Special Education Core Skills (Birth to Age 21): Teacher Certification /
   Sharon A. Wynne. -1st ed.
   ISBN: 978-1-60787-083-8
   1. Minnesota Special Education Core Skills (Birth to Age 21).   2. Study Guides
   3. MTLE   4. Teachers' Certification & Licensure   5. Careers

Disclaimer:

The opinions expressed in this publication are the sole works of XAMonline and were created independently from the National Education Association, Educational Testing Service, or any State Department of Education, National Evaluation Systems or other testing affiliates.

Between the time of publication and printing, state specific standards as well as testing formats and website information may change that is not included in part or in whole within this product. Sample test questions are developed by XAMonline and reflect similar content as on real tests; however, they are not former tests. XAMonline assembles content that aligns with state standards but makes no claims nor guarantees teacher candidates a passing score. Numerical scores are determined by testing companies such as NES or ETS and then are compared with individual state standards. A passing score varies from state to state.

Printed in the United States of America   œ-1

Minnesota Special Education Core Skills (Birth to Age 21)
ISBN: 978-1-60787-083-8

TABLE OF CONTENTS

DOMAIN I   **UNDERSTANDING STUDENTS WITH DISABILITIES**

COMPETENCY 001   **UNDERSTAND THE VARIOUS CHARACTERISTICS AND NEEDS OF STUDENTS WITH DISABILITIES**

Skill 1.1   Demonstrating knowledge of typical and atypical human growth and development in various domains (e.g., cognitive, physical, social, emotional, communicative) 1

Skill 1.2   Demonstrating knowledge of the types, etiology, identification criteria, characteristics, and continuum of severity of various disabilities 15

Skill 1.3   Demonstrating familiarity with similarities and differences among individuals with disabilities, including those with coexisting disabilities 20

COMPETENCY 002   **UNDERSTAND FACTORS THAT AFFECT DEVELOPMENT AND LEARNING IN STUDENTS WITH DISABILITIES**

Skill 2.1   Recognizing the educational implications of various types of disabilities, including coexisting disabilities 23

Skill 2.2   Demonstrating knowledge of the roles families play in supporting students' development and learning 23

Skill 2.3   Demonstrating knowledge of the lifelong impact of disabilities on students and their families 24

Skill 2.4   Recognizing ways in which teacher attitudes, behaviors, and cultural competence affect individuals with disabilities 25

Skill 2.5   Demonstrating familiarity with the general effects of various types of medications (e.g., anti-seizure, stimulant, antidepressant) on the educational, cognitive, physical, social, and emotional behavior of individuals with disabilities 27

DOMAIN II   **ASSESSING STUDENTS AND DEVELOPING PROGRAMS**

COMPETENCY 003   **UNDERSTAND PROCEDURES FOR SELECTING AND ADMINISTERING VARIOUS TYPES OF ASSESSMENTS TO ADDRESS THE INDIVIDUAL NEEDS OF STUDENTS WITH DISABILITIES**

Skill 3.1   Recognizing the uses and limitations of various formal and informal assessments (e.g., statewide achievement tests, intelligence tests, observations, behavior rating scales, inventories) 30

Skill 3.2   Demonstrating knowledge of screening, pre-referral, referral, and eligibility procedures (e.g., to address a student's academic functioning and/or mental health needs) 32

Skill 3.3   Demonstrating knowledge of how to select and administer comprehensive, unbiased formal and informal assessments, including assessments of students from culturally and linguistically diverse backgrounds 36

COMPETENCY 004   **UNDERSTAND STRATEGIES AND PROCEDURES FOR DEVELOPING, IMPLEMENTING, AND MONITORING INDIVIDUALIZED EDUCATION PROGRAMS (IEPS) AND TRANSITION PLANS**

Skill 4.1   Demonstrating knowledge of how to interpret and communicate the results of formal and informal assessments to students, families, teachers, and other professionals and recommend appropriate services and interventions based on those results 39

Skill 4.2   Recognizing the continuum of placements and services available for students with disabilities 39

Skill 4.3   Demonstrating knowledge of how to use assessment information to make appropriate eligibility, program, and placement recommendations for students with disabilities, including those from culturally and linguistically diverse backgrounds 41

Skill 4.4   Demonstrating knowledge of procedures for establishing case records, including how to write assessment team summaries, technically sound IEPs, transition plans, and behavioral plans 43

Skill 4.5   Demonstrating knowledge of systematic procedures for compiling data on a student or group of students for the purpose of continuous program evaluation and improvement 47

DOMAIN III   **PROMOTING STUDENT DEVELOPMENT AND LEARNING**

COMPETENCY 005   **UNDERSTAND STRATEGIES AND PROCEDURES FOR PLANNING, MANAGING, AND MODIFYING THE LEARNING ENVIRONMENT FOR STUDENTS WITH DISABILITIES, INCLUDING STRATEGIES FOR BEHAVIOR MANAGEMENT**

Skill 5.1   Applying knowledge of strategies for teaching students with disabilities in a variety of environments (e.g., one-on-one setting, small group, general education classroom) 49

Skill 5.2   Demonstrating knowledge of strategies for planning and managing the learning environment for students with disabilities (e.g., fostering students' independence, designing consistent daily routines, establishing behavioral expectations, maintaining students' attention)52

Skill 5.3   Applying knowledge of strategies for developing, implementing, modifying, and monitoring classroom behavior management plans for students with disabilities, including strategies for providing individual and school-wide positive behavioral supports 57

Skill 5.4   Demonstrating knowledge of strategies for crisis intervention and prevention.. 63

COMPETENCY 006   **UNDERSTAND EFFECTIVE CURRICULAR PLANNING AND INSTRUCTIONAL PRACTICES FOR STUDENTS WITH DISABILITIES**

Skill 6.1   Applying knowledge of how to adapt and modify the general and special education curricula to meet the individual needs of students with disabilities (e.g., providing access to the general curriculum; incorporating functional living, communication, and/or social skills) 66

Skill 6.2   Applying knowledge of how to monitor, adapt, and modify instruction to meet the individual needs of students with disabilities (e.g., using remedial methods to provide additional instruction and practice, providing accommodations such as assistive technologies, conducting and using task analysis to sequence instruction, using methods to foster students' independence).. 69

DOMAIN IV   **WORKING IN A PROFESSIONAL ENVIRONMENT**

COMPETENCY 007   **UNDERSTAND THE HISTORICAL, PHILOSOPHICAL, AND LEGAL FOUNDATIONS OF THE FIELD OF SPECIAL EDUCATION**

Skill 7.1   Demonstrating knowledge of the historical and philosophical foundations of special education and contemporary issues pertaining to the education of individuals with disabilities, including the roles and organizational structures of general and special education and the parts they play in providing total services to all students 79

Skill 7.2   Applying knowledge of the legal bases and ethical guidelines pertaining to the education of students with disabilities (e.g., rights and responsibilities of students, parents/guardians, teachers, and schools; due process and procedural safeguards; data privacy requirements; assessment procedures; guidelines related to behavior management)94

COMPETENCY 008   **UNDERSTAND HOW TO COMMUNICATE AND COLLABORATE WITH OTHERS TO HELP STUDENTS WITH DISABILITIES ACHIEVE DESIRED LEARNING OUTCOMES**

Skill 8.1   Demonstrating knowledge of family systems theory and the roles of parents/guardians in the educational process (e.g., serving as primary informal teachers of their children; collaborating in designing, implementing, and evaluating IEPs, transition plans, and behavioral plans).. 99

Skill 8.2   Demonstrating knowledge of how to assist parents/guardians in identifying resources in relation to their children's development and education.. 100

Skill 8.3   Applying knowledge of effective strategies for communicating, collaborating, and consulting with general education teachers, related services providers, other school staff members, medical professionals, and representatives of community agencies to provide services for students with disabilities and their families (e.g., providing learning opportunities, adapting and modifying curriculum and instruction, addressing mental health needs, engaging in transition planning) ... 103

Skill 8.4   Demonstrating knowledge of effective strategies for supervising, monitoring, and evaluating the activities of paraprofessionals, aides, volunteers, and peer tutors... 105

Skill 8.5   Applying knowledge of small-group processes and effective strategies for facilitating child study teams, IEP-planning teams, and transition-planning teams 108

Sample Test 111

Answer Key 136

Rigor Table 137

Rationales 138

Section 1 About XAMonline

XAMonline – A Specialty Teacher Certification Company

Created in 1996, XAMonline was the first company to publish study guides for state-specific teacher certification examinations. Founder Sharon Wynne found it frustrating that materials were not available for teacher certification preparation and decided to create the first single, state-specific guide. XAMonline has grown into a company of over 1800 contributors and writers and offers over 300 titles for the entire PRAXIS series and every state examination. No matter what state you plan on teaching in, XAMonline has a unique teacher certification study guide just for you.

XAMonline – Value and Innovation

We are committed to providing value and innovation. Our print-on-demand technology allows us to be the first in the market to reflect changes in test standards and user feedback as they occur. Our guides are written by experienced teachers who are experts in their fields. And, our content reflects the highest standards of quality. Comprehensive practice tests with varied levels of rigor means that your study experience will closely match the actual in-test experience.

To date, XAMonline has helped nearly 600,000 teachers pass their certification or licensing exams. Our commitment to preparation exceeds simply providing the proper material for study - it extends to helping teachers **gain mastery** of the subject matter, giving them the **tools** to become the most effective classroom leaders possible, and ushering today's students toward a **successful future**.

Section 2 About this Study Guide

Purpose of this Guide
Is there a little voice inside of you saying, "Am I ready?" Our goal is to replace that little voice and remove all doubt with a new voice that says, "I AM READY. **Bring it on**!" by offering the highest quality of teacher certification study guides.

Organization of Content
You will see that while every test may start with overlapping general topics, each are very unique in the skills they wish to test. Only XAMonline presents custom content that analyzes deeper than a title, a subarea, or an objective. Only XAMonline presents content and sample test assessments along with **focus statements**, the deepest-level rationale and interpretation of the skills that are unique to the exam.

Title and field number of test
→Each exam has its own name and number. XAMonline's guides are written to give you the content you need to know for the <u>specific</u> exam you are taking. You can be confident when you buy our guide that it contains the information you need to study for the specific test you are taking.

Subareas
→These are the major content categories found on the exam. XAMonline's guides are written to cover all of the subareas found in the test frameworks developed for the exam.

Objectives
→These are standards that are unique to the exam and represent the main subcategories of the subareas/content categories. XAMonline's guides are written to address every specific objective required to pass the exam.

Focus statements
→These are examples and interpretations of the objectives. You find them in parenthesis directly following the objective. They provide detailed examples of the range, type, and level of content that appear on the test questions. **Only XAMonline's guides drill down to this level.**

How do We Compare with Our Competitors?
XAMonline – drills down to the focus statement level
CliffsNotes and REA – organized at the objective level
Kaplan – provides only links to content
MoMedia – content not specific to the test

Each subarea is divided into manageable sections that cover the specific skill areas. Explanations are easy-to-understand and thorough. You'll find that every test answer contains a rejoinder so if you need a refresher or further review after taking the test, you'll know exactly to which section you must return.

How to Use this Book

Our informal polls show that most people begin studying up to 8 weeks prior to the test date, so start early. Then ask yourself some questions: How much do you really know? Are you coming to the test straight from your teacher-education program or are you having to review subjects you haven't considered in 10 years? Either way, take a **diagnostic or assessment test** first. Also, spend time on sample tests so that you become accustomed to the way the actual test will appear.

This guide comes with an online diagnostic test of 30 questions found online at www.XAMonline.com. It is a little boot camp to get you up for the task and reveal things about your compendium of knowledge in general. Although this guide is structured to follow the order of the test, you are not required to study in that order. By finding a time-management and study plan that fits your life you will be more effective. The results of your diagnostic or self-assessment test can be a guide for how to manage your time and point you towards an area that needs more attention.

After taking the diagnostic exam, fill out the **Personalized Study Plan** page at the beginning of each chapter. Review the competencies and skills covered in that chapter and check the boxes that apply to your study needs. If there are sections you already know you can skip, check the "skip it" box. Taking this step will give you a study plan for each chapter.

Week	Activity
8 weeks prior to test	Take a diagnostic test found at www.XAMonline.com
7 weeks prior to test	Build your Personalized Study Plan for each chapter. Check the "skip it" box for sections you feel you are already strong in.
6-3 weeks prior to test	For each of these 4 weeks, choose a content area to study. You don't have to go in the order of the book. It may be that you start with the content that needs the most review. Alternately, you may want to ease yourself into plan by starting with the most familiar material.
2 weeks prior to test	Take the sample test, score it, and create a review plan for the final week before the test.
1 week prior to test	Following your plan (which will likely be aligned with the areas that need the most review) go back and study the sections that align with the questions you may have gotten wrong. Then go back and study the sections related to the questions you answered correctly. If need be, create flashcards and drill yourself on any area that you makes you anxious.

Section 3 About the Minnesota Special Education Core Skills (Birth to Age 21) Exam

What is the Minnesota Special Education Core Skills (Birth to Age 21) Exam?
The Minnesota Special Education Core Skills (Birth to Age 21) exam is meant to assess mastery of the knowledge and skills required to teach special education students in Minnesota public schools.

Often **your own state's requirements** determine whether or not you should take any particular test. The most reliable source of information regarding this is your state's Department of Education. This resource should have a complete list of testing centers and dates. Test dates vary by subject area and not all test dates necessarily include your particular test, so be sure to check carefully.

If you are in a teacher-education program, check with the Education Department or the Certification Officer for specific information for testing and testing timelines. The Certification Office should have most of the information you need.

If you choose an alternative route to certification you can either rely on our website at www.XAMonline.com or on the resources provided by an alternative certification program. Many states now have specific agencies devoted to alternative certification and there are some national organizations as well, for example:
National Association for Alternative Certification
http://www.alt-teachercert.org/index.asp

Interpreting Test Results
Contrary to what you may have heard, the results of the Minnesota Special Education Core Skills (Birth to Age 21) test are not based on time. More accurately, your score will be based on the raw number of points you earn in each section, the proportion of that section to the entire subtest, and the scaling of the raw score. Raw scores are converted to a scale of 100 to 300. It is likely to your benefit to complete as many questions in the time allotted, but it will not necessarily work to your advantage if you hurry through the test.

Scores are available by email if you request this when you register. Score reports are available 21days after the testing window and posted to your account for 45 days as PDFs. Scores will also be sent to your chosen institution(s).

What's on the Test?
The Minnesota Special Education Core Skills (Birth to Age 21) exam is a computer-based test and consists of two subtests, each lasting one hour. You can take one or both subtests at one testing appointment. The breakdown of the questions is as follows:

Category	Approximate Number of Questions	Approximate Percentage of the test
SUBTEST 1	50	
I: Understanding Students with Disabilities		50%
II: Assessing Students and Developing Programs		50%
SUBTEST 2	50	
I: Promoting Student Development and Learning		50%
II: Working in a Professional Environment		50%

Question Types

You're probably thinking, enough already, I want to study! Indulge us a little longer while we explain that there is actually more than one type of multiple-choice question. You can thank us later after you realize how well prepared you are for your exam.

1. **Complete the Statement.** The name says it all. In this question type you'll be asked to choose the correct completion of a given statement. For example: The Dolch Basic Sight Words consist of a relatively short list of words that children should be able to:
    a. Sound out
    b. Know the meaning of
    c. Recognize on sight
    d. Use in a sentence

    The correct answer is C. In order to check your answer, test out the statement by adding the choices to the end of it.

2. **Which of the Following.** One way to test your answer choice for this type of question is to replace the phrase "which of the following" with your selection. Use this example: Which of the following words is one of the twelve most frequently used in children's reading texts:
    a. There
    b. This
    c. The
    d. An

    Don't look! Test your answer. _____ is one of the twelve most frequently used in children's reading texts. Did you guess C? Then you guessed correctly.

3. **Roman Numeral Choices.** This question type is used when there is more than one possible correct answer. For example: Which of the following two arguments accurately supports the use of cooperative learning as an effective method of instruction?

I. Cooperative learning groups facilitate healthy competition between individuals in the group.
II. Cooperative learning groups allow academic achievers to carry or cover for academic underachievers.
III. Cooperative learning groups make each student in the group accountable for the success of the group.
IV. Cooperative learning groups make it possible for students to reward other group members for achieving.

      A. I and II
      B. II and III
      C. I and III
      D. III and IV

Notice that the question states there are **two** possible answers. It's best to read all the possibilities first before looking at the answer choices. In this case, the correct answer is D.

4. **Negative Questions.** This type of question contains words such as "not," "least," and "except." Each correct answer will be the statement that does **not** fit the situation described in the question. Such as: Multicultural education is **not**

    a. An idea or concept
    b. A "tack-on" to the school curriculum
    c. An educational reform movement
    d. A process

Think to yourself that the statement could be anything but the correct answer. This question form is more open to interpretation than other types, so read carefully and don't forget that you're answering a negative statement.

5. **Questions That Include Graphs, Tables, or Reading Passages.** As ever, read the question carefully. It likely asks for a very specific answer and not broad interpretation of the visual. Here is a simple (though not statistically accurate) example of a graph question: In the following graph in how many years did more men take the NYSTCE exam than women?

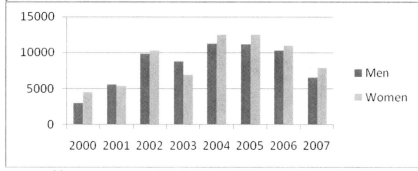

    a. None
    b. One
    c. Two
    d. Three

It may help you to simply circle the two years that answer the question. Make sure you've read the question thoroughly and once you've made your determination, double check your work. The correct answer is C.

Section 4 Helpful Hints

Study Tips

1. **You are what you eat.** Certain foods aid the learning process by releasing natural memory enhancers called CCKs (cholecystokinin) composed of tryptophan, choline, and phenylalanine. All of these chemicals enhance the neurotransmitters associated with memory and certain foods release memory enhancing chemicals. A light meal or snacks from the following foods fall into this category:
   - Milk
   - Nuts and seeds
   - Rice
   - Oats
   - Eggs
   - Turkey
   - Fish

   The better the connections, the more you comprehend!

2. **See the forest for the trees.** In other words, get the concept before you look at the details. One way to do this is to take notes as you read, paraphrasing or summarizing in your own words. Putting the concept in terms that are comfortable and familiar may increase retention.

3. **Question authority.** Ask why, why, why. Pull apart written material paragraph by paragraph and don't forget the captions under the illustrations. For example, if a heading reads *Stream Erosion* put it in the form of a question (why do streams erode? Or what is stream erosion?) then find the answer within the material. If you train your mind to think in this manner you will learn more and prepare yourself for answering test questions.

4. **Play mind games.** Using your brain for reading or puzzles keeps it flexible. Even with a limited amount of time your brain can take in data (much like a computer) and store it for later use. In ten minutes you can: read two paragraphs (at least), quiz yourself with flash cards, or review notes. Even if you don't fully understand something on the first pass, your mind stores it for recall, which is why frequent reading or review increases chances of retention and comprehension.

5. **The pen is mightier than the sword.** Learn to take great notes. A by-product of our modern culture is that we have grown accustomed to getting our information in short doses. We've subconsciously trained ourselves to assimilate information into neat little packages. Messy notes fragment the flow of information. Your notes can be much clearer with proper formatting. *The Cornell Method* is one such format. This method was popularized in *How to Study in College,* Ninth Edition, by Walter Pauk. You can benefit from the method without purchasing an additional book by simply looking the

method up online. Below is a sample of how *The Cornell Method* can be adapted for use with this guide.

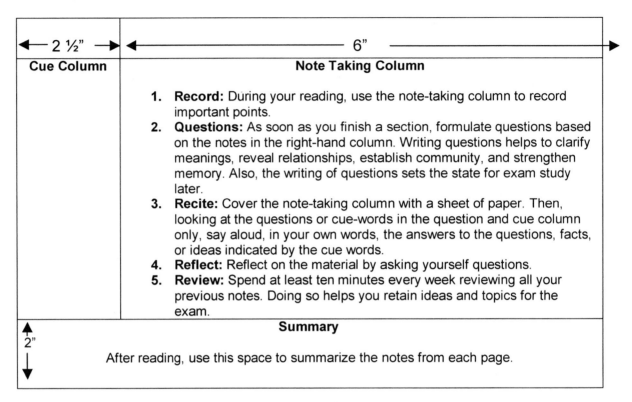

← 2 ½" →	← ——————————— 6" ——————————— →
Cue Column	**Note Taking Column**
	1. **Record:** During your reading, use the note-taking column to record important points.
	2. **Questions:** As soon as you finish a section, formulate questions based on the notes in the right-hand column. Writing questions helps to clarify meanings, reveal relationships, establish community, and strengthen memory. Also, the writing of questions sets the state for exam study later.
	3. **Recite:** Cover the note-taking column with a sheet of paper. Then, looking at the questions or cue-words in the question and cue column only, say aloud, in your own words, the answers to the questions, facts, or ideas indicated by the cue words.
	4. **Reflect:** Reflect on the material by asking yourself questions.
	5. **Review:** Spend at least ten minutes every week reviewing all your previous notes. Doing so helps you retain ideas and topics for the exam.
↕ 2"	**Summary**
	After reading, use this space to summarize the notes from each page.

*Adapted from *How to Study in College,* Ninth Edition, by Walter Pauk, ©2008 Wadsworth

6. **Place yourself in exile and set the mood.** Set aside a particular place and time to study that best suits your personal needs and biorhythms. If you're a night person, burn the midnight oil. If you're a morning person set yourself up with some coffee and get to it. Make your study time and place as free from distraction as possible and surround yourself with what you need, be it silence or music. Studies have shown that music can aid in concentration, absorption, and retrieval of information. Not all music, though. Classical music is said to work best.

7. **Get pointed in the right direction.** Use arrows to point to important passages or pieces of information. It's easier to read than a page full of yellow highlights. Highlighting can be used sparingly, but add an arrow to the margin to call attention to it.

8. **Check your budget.** You should at least review all the content material before your test, but allocate the most amount of time to the areas that need the most refreshing. It sounds obvious, but it's easy to forget. You can use the study rubric above to balance your study budget.

Testing Tips

1. **Get smart, play dumb.** Sometimes a question is just a question. No one is out to trick you, so don't assume that the test writer is looking for something other than what was asked. Stick to the question as written and don't overanalyze.

2. **Do a double take.** Read test questions and answer choices at least twice because it's easy to miss something, to transpose a word or some letters. If you have no idea what the correct answer is, skip it and come back later if there's time. If you're still clueless, it's okay to guess. Remember, you're scored on the number of questions you answer correctly and you're not penalized for wrong answers. The worst case scenario is that you miss a point from a good guess.

3. **Turn it on its ear.** The syntax of a question can often provide a clue, so make things interesting and turn the question into a statement to see if it changes the meaning or relates better (or worse) to the answer choices.

4. **Get out your magnifying glass.** Look for hidden clues in the questions because it's difficult to write a multiple-choice question without giving away part of the answer in the options presented. In most questions you can readily eliminate one or two potential answers, increasing your chances of answering correctly to 50/50, which will help out if you've skipped a question and gone back to it (see tip #2).

5. **Call it intuition.** Often your first instinct is correct. If you've been studying the content you've likely absorbed something and have subconsciously retained the knowledge. On questions you're not sure about trust your instincts because a first impression is usually correct.

6. **Graffiti.** Sometimes it's a good idea to mark your answers directly on the test booklet and go back to fill in the optical scan sheet later. You don't get extra points for perfectly blackened ovals. If you choose to manage your test this way, be sure not to mismark your answers when you transcribe to the scan sheet.

7. **Become a clock-watcher.** You have a set amount of time to answer the questions. Don't get bogged down laboring over a question you're not sure about when there are ten others you could answer more readily. If you choose to follow the advice of tip #6, be sure you leave time near the end to go back and fill in the scan sheet.

The proctor will write the start time where it can be seen and then, later, provide the time remaining, typically 15 minutes before the end of the test.

Do the Drill

No matter how prepared you feel it's sometimes a good idea to apply Murphy's Law. So the following tips might seem silly, mundane, or obvious, but we're including them anyway.

1. **Remember, you are what you eat, so bring a snack.** Choose from the list of energizing foods that appear earlier in the introduction.

2. **You're not too sexy for your test.** Wear comfortable clothes. You'll be distracted if your belt is too tight, or if you're too cold or too hot.

3. **Lie to yourself.** Even if you think you're a prompt person, pretend you're not and leave plenty of time to get to the testing center. Map it out ahead of time and do a dry run if you have to. There's no need to add road rage to your list of anxieties.

4. **Bring sharp, number 2 pencils.** It may seem impossible to forget this need from your school days, but you might. And make sure the erasers are intact, too.

5. **No ticket, no test.** Bring your admission ticket as well as **two** forms of identification, including one with a picture and signature. You will not be admitted to the test without these things.

6. **You can't take it with you.** Leave any study aids, dictionaries, notebooks, computers and the like at home. Certain tests **do** allow a scientific or four-function calculator, so check ahead of time if your test does.

7. **Prepare for the desert.** Any time spent on a bathroom break **cannot** be made up later, so use your judgment on the amount you eat or drink.

8. **Quiet, Please!** Keeping your own time is a good idea, but not with a timepiece that has a loud ticker. If you use a watch, take it off and place it nearby but not so that it distracts you. And **silence your cell phone.**

To the best of our ability, we have compiled the content you need to know in this book and in the accompanying online resources. The rest is up to you. You can use the study and testing tips or you can follow your own methods. Either way, you can be confident that there aren't any missing pieces of information and there shouldn't be any surprises in the content on the test.

If you have questions about test fees, registration, electronic testing, or other content verification issues please visit www.mtle.nesinc.com.

Good luck!
Sharon Wynne
Founder, XAMonline

DOMAIN I   **UNDERSTANDING STUDENTS WITH DISABILITIES**

COMPETENCY 001   **UNDERSTAND THE VARIOUS CHARACTERISTICS AND NEEDS OF STUDENTS WITH DISABILITIES**

Skill 1.1   **Demonstrating knowledge of typical and atypical human growth and development in various domains (e.g., cognitive, physical, social, emotional, communicative)**

SOCIAL EMOTIONAL

This topic pertains to children whose behavior deviates from society's standards for normal behavior for certain ages and stages of development. Behavioral expectations vary from setting to setting—for example, it is acceptable to yell on the football field but not when the teacher is explaining a lesson to the class. Different cultures have their own standards of behavior, further complicating the question of what constitutes a behavioral problem. People also have their personal opinions and standards for what is tolerable and what is not. Some behavioral problems are openly expressed; others are inwardly directed and not very obvious. As a result of these factors, the terms *behavioral disorders* and *emotional disturbance* have become almost interchangeable.

While almost all children will at some time exhibit behaviors that are aggressive, withdrawn, or otherwise inappropriate, the IDEA definition of serious emotional disturbance focuses on behaviors that persist over time, are intense, and impair a child's ability to function in society. The behaviors defined by IDEA must be those not caused by temporary stressful situations or other events (e.g., depression over the death of a grandparent or anger over the parents' impending divorce). In order for a child to be considered seriously emotionally disturbed, he or she must exhibit one or more of the following characteristics over a *long period of time* and to a *marked degree* that *adversely affects* the child's educational performance:

- Inability to learn, which cannot be explained by intellectual, sensory, or health factors
- Inability to maintain satisfactory interpersonal relationships
- Inappropriate types of behaviors
- General pervasive mood of unhappiness or depression
- Physical symptoms or fears associated with personal or school problems

Schizophrenic children are covered under this definition, and social maladjustment by itself does not satisfy this definition unless it is accompanied by one of the other conditions of SED.

The diagnostic categories and definitions used to classify mental disorders come from the American Psychiatric Association's publication, *Diagnostic and Statistical Manual of Mental Disorders* (DSM-IV), the handbook that is used by psychiatrists and psychologists. The DSM-IV is a multiaxial classification system consisting of dimensions (axes) coded along with the psychiatric diagnosis. The axes are:

- Axis I   Principal psychiatric diagnosis (e.g., overanxious disorder)
- Axis II   Developmental problems (e.g., developmental reading disorder)
- Axis III   Physical disorders (e.g., allergies)
- Axis IV   Psychosocial stressors (e.g., divorce)
- Axis V   Rating of the highest level of adaptive functioning (includes intellectual and social). Rating is called Global Assessment Functioning (GAF) score.

While the DSM-IV diagnosis is one way of diagnosing serious emotional disturbance, there are other ways of classifying the various forms by which behavior disorders manifest themselves. The following tables summarize some of these classifications.

Externalizing Behaviors	Internalizing Behaviors
Aggressive behaviors expressed outwardly toward others	Withdrawing behaviors that are directed inward to oneself
Manifested as hyperactivity, persistent aggression, and irritating behaviors that are impulsive and distractible	Social withdrawal
Examples: hitting, cursing, stealing, arson, cruelty to animals, hyperactivity,	Depression, fears, phobias, elective mutism, withdrawal, anorexia, and bulimia

Well-known instruments used to assess children's behavior have their own categories (scales) to classify behaviors. The following table illustrates the scales of some of the widely used instruments.

Walker Problem Identification Checklist	Burks' Behavior Rating Scales (BBRS)	Devereux Behavior Rating Scale (adolescent)	Revised Behavior Problem Checklist (Quay & Peterson)
Acting out	Excessive self-blame	Unethical behavior	Major scales
Withdrawal	Excessive anxiety	Defiant-resistive	Conduct Disorder
Distractibility	Excessive withdrawal	Domineering-sadistic	Socialized aggression
Disturbed peer Relations	Excessive dependency	Heterosexual interest	Attention-problems-immaturity
Immaturity	Poor ego strength	Hyperactive expansive	Anxiety-withdrawal
	Poor physical strength	Poor emotional control	
	Poor coordination	Needs approval, dependency	Minor scales
	Poor intellectuality	Emotional disturbance	Psychotic behavior
	Poor academics	Physical inferiority-timidity	Motor excess
	Poor attention	Schizoid withdrawal	
	Poor impulse control	Bizarre speech and cognition	
	Poor reality contact	Bizarre actions	
	Poor sense of identity		
	Excessive suffering		
	Poor anger control		
	Excessive sense of persecution		
	Excessive aggressiveness		
	Excessive resistance		
	Poor social conformity		

Disturbance may also be categorized in degrees: mild, moderate, or severe. The degree of disturbance will affect the type and degree of interventions and services required by emotionally handicapped students. Degree of disturbance must also be considered when determining the least restrictive environment and appropriate education. One example of a set of criteria for determining the degree of disturbance is that developed by P.L. Newcomer:

Criteria	Degree of Disturbance		
	Mild	**Moderate**	**Severe**
Precipitating events	Highly stressful	Moderately stressful	Not stressful
Destructiveness	Not destructive	Occasionally destructive	Usually destructive
Maturational appropriateness	Behavior typical for age	Some behavior untypical for age	Behavior too young or too old
Personal functioning	Cares for own needs	Usually cares for own needs	Unable to care for own needs
Social functioning	Usually able to relate to others	Usually unable to relate to others	Unable to relate to others
Reality index	Usually sees events as they are	Occasionally sees events as they are	Little contact with reality
Insight index	Aware of behavior	Usually aware of behavior	Usually not aware of behavior
Conscious control	Usually can control behavior	Occasionally can control behavior	Little control over behavior
Social responsiveness	Usually acts appropriately	Occasionally acts appropriately	Rarely acts appropriately

Source: *Understanding and Teaching Emotionally Disturbed Children and Adolescents*, (2nd ed., p. 139), by P.L. Newcomer, 1993, Austin, TX: Pro-De. Copyright 1993. Reprinted with permission.

LANGUAGE DEVELOPMENT AND BEHAVIOR

Language is the means whereby people communicate their thoughts, make requests, and respond to others. Communication competence is an interaction of cognitive competence, social knowledge, and language competence. Communication problems may result from any or all of these areas that directly impact the student's ability to interact with others. Language consists of several components, each of which follows a sequence of development.

Brown and colleagues were the first to describe language as a function of developmental stages rather than age. Brown developed a formula to group the mean length of utterances (sentences) into stages. Counting the number of morphemes per 100 utterances, one can calculate a mean length of utterance (MLU). Total number of morphemes / 100 = MLU (e.g. 180/100 = 1.8).

Summary of Brown's Findings about MLU and Language Development:

Stage	MLU	Developmental Features
L	1.5–2.0	14 basic morphemes (e.g., in, on, articles, possessives)
LI	2.0–2.5	Beginning of pronoun use, auxiliary verbs
LII	2.5–3.0	Language forms approximate adult forms, beginning of questions and negative statements
Lv	3.0–3.5	Use of complex (embedded) sentences
V	3.5–4.0	Use of compound sentences

COMPONENTS OF LANGUAGE

Language learning is made up of five components. Children progress through developmental stages through each component.

Phonology

Phonology is the system of rules about sounds and sound combinations for a language. A phoneme is the smallest unit of sound that combines with other sounds to make words. A phoneme, by itself, does not have a meaning; it must be combined with other phonemes. Problems in phonology may be manifested as developmental delays in acquiring consonants or as reception problems, such as misinterpreting words because a different consonant was substituted.

Morphology

Morphemes are the smallest units of language that convey meaning. Morphemes are root words—free morphemes that can stand alone (e.g., walk) and affixes (e.g., -ed, -s, -ing). Content words carry the meaning in a sentence, and functional words join phrases and sentences. Generally, students with problems in this area may not use inflectional endings in their words, may not be consistent in their use of certain morphemes, or may be delayed in learning morphemes, such as irregular past tenses.

Syntax

Syntax rules, commonly known as grammar, govern how morphemes and words are correctly combined. Wood (1976) describes six stages of syntax acquisition:

- **Stages 1 and 2** - Birth to about 2 years: child is learning the semantic system.
- **Stage 3** - Ages 2 to 3 years: simple sentences contain subject and predicate.
- **Stage 4** - Ages 2 ½ to 4 years: elements such as question words are added to basic sentences (e.g., where), and word order is changed to ask questions. The child begins to use "and" to combine simple sentences, and embeds words within the basic sentence.
- **Stage 5** - Ages 3 ½ to 7 years: the child uses complete sentences that include word classes of adult language. The child is becoming aware of appropriate semantic functions of words and differences within the same grammatical classes.
- **Stage 6** - Ages 5 to 20 years: the child begins to learn complex sentences and sentences that imply commands, requests, and promises.

Syntactic deficits are manifested when the child uses sentences that lack length or complexity that are average for a child that age. The child may have problems understanding or creating complex sentences and embedded sentences.

Semantics

Semantics is language content: objects, actions, and relations between objects. As with syntax, Wood (1976) outlines stages of semantic development:

- **Stage 1** - Birth to about 2 years: the child is learning meaning while learning his or her first words. Sentences are one word, but the meaning varies according to the context. Therefore, "doggie" may mean, "This is my dog," or "There is a dog," or "The dog is barking."
- **Stage 2** - About 2 to 8 years: the child progresses to two-word sentences about concrete actions. As more words are learned, the child forms longer sentences; until about age 7, things are defined in terms of visible actions. The child begins to respond to prompts (e.g., pretty/flower). At about age 8, the child can respond to a prompt with an opposite (e.g., pretty/ugly).
- **Stage 3** - Begins at about age 8: the child's word meanings relate directly to experiences, operations, and processes. Vocabulary is defined by the child's experiences, not the adult's. At about age 12, the child begins to give "dictionary" definitions, and the semantic level approaches that of adults.

Semantic problems take the form of:

- Limited vocabulary
- Inability to understand figurative language or idioms; interprets literally
- Failure to perceive multiple meanings of words and changes in word meaning from changes in context, resulting in incomplete understanding of what is read

- Difficulty understanding linguistic concepts (e.g., before/after), verbal analogies, and logical relationships, such as possessives, spatial, and temporal
- Misuse of transitional words such as "although" and "regardless"

Pragmatics

Commonly known as the speaker's intent, pragmatics are used to influence or control the actions or attitudes of others. *Communicative competence* depends on how well one understands the rules of language, as well as the social rules of communication, such as taking turns and using the correct tone of voice.

Pragmatic deficits are manifested by failures to respond properly to indirect requests after age 8 (e.g., "Can't you turn down the TV?" elicits a response of "No" instead of "Yes" when the child turns down the volume). Children with these deficits have trouble reading cues that indicate the listener does not understand them. Whereas a person would usually notice this and adjust his or her speech to the listener's needs, the child with pragmatic problems does not do this.

Pragmatic deficits are also characterized by inappropriate social behaviors, such as interrupting or monopolizing conversations. Children may use immature speech and have trouble sticking to a topic. These problems can persist into adulthood, affecting academic, vocational, and social interactions.

Problems in language development often require long-term interventions and can persist into adulthood. Certain problems are associated with different grade levels:

- **Preschool and kindergarten**: The child's speech may sound immature. He or she may not be able to follow simple directions and often cannot name things such as the days of the week or colors. The child may not be able to discriminate between sounds and the letters associated with the sounds. The child might substitute sounds and have trouble responding accurately to certain types of questions. The child may play less with his or her peers or participate in nonplay or parallel play.
- **Elementary school**: Problems with sound discrimination persist, and the child may have problems with temporal and spatial concepts (e.g., before/after). As the child progresses through school, he or she may have problems making the transition from narrative to expository writing. Word retrieval problems may not be very evident because the child begins to devise strategies (such as talking around the word he or she cannot remember, or using fillers and descriptors). The child might speak more slowly, have problems sounding out words, and get confused with multiple-meaning words. Pragmatic problems—failure to correctly interpret social cues and adjust to appropriate language, inability to predict consequences, and inability to formulate requests to obtain new information—show up in social situations.

- **Secondary school**: At this level, difficulties become more subtle. The child lacks the ability to use and understand higher-level syntax, semantics, and pragmatics. If the child has problems with auditory language, he or she may also have problems with short-term memory. Receptive and/or expressive language delays impair the child's ability to learn effectively. The child often lacks the ability to organize/categorize the information received in school. Problems associated with pragmatic deficiencies persist; because the child is aware of them, he or she becomes inattentive, withdrawn, or frustrated.

COGNITIVE DEVELOPMENT

Children go through patterns of learning, beginning with pre-operational thought processes, and move to concrete operational thoughts. Eventually, they begin to acquire the mental ability to think about and solve problems in their heads because they can manipulate objects symbolically. Children of most ages can use symbols (such as words and numbers) to represent objects and relations, but they need concrete reference points. It is essential that children be encouraged to use and develop the thinking skills they possess in solving problems that interest them. The content of the curriculum must be relevant, engaging, and meaningful to the students.

The teacher of special needs students must have a general knowledge of cognitive development. Although children with cognitive development special needs may be different than other children, a teacher needs to be aware of some of the activities of each stage as part of the basis to determine what should be taught and when.

The following information about cognitive development was taken from the Cincinnati Children's Hospital Medical Center at www.cincinnatichildrens.org. Some common features indicating a progression from simple to more complex cognitive development include the following:

Children (ages 6-12)
Begin to develop the ability to think in concrete ways. Concrete operations are operations performed in the presence of the object and events that are to be used.

Examples: how to combine (addition), separate (subtract or divide), order (alphabetize and sort/categorize), and transform (25 pennies=1 quarter) objects and actions

Adolescence (ages 12-18)
Adolescence marks the beginning of the development of more complex thinking skills, including abstract thinking, the ability to reason from known principles (form own new ideas or questions), the ability to consider many points of view according to varying criteria (compare or debate ideas or opinions), and the ability to think about the process of thinking.

What cognitive developmental changes occur during adolescence?

During adolescence, the developing teenager acquires the ability to think *systematically* about all logical relationships within a problem. The transition from concrete thinking to formal logical operations occurs over time. Every adolescent progresses at a varying rate in developing his or her ability to think in more complex ways. Each adolescent develops his or her own view of the world. Some adolescents may be able to apply logical operations to school work long before they are able to apply them to personal dilemmas. When emotional issues arise, they often interfere with an adolescent's ability to think in more complex ways. The ability to consider possibilities as well as facts may influence decision making in either positive or negative ways.

Here are some common features indicating a progression from more simple to more complex cognitive development:

Early adolescence

During early adolescence, the use of more complex thinking is focused on personal decision making in school and home environments, including the following:

- Begins to demonstrate use of formal logical operations in school work
- Begins to question authority and society standards
- Begins to form and verbalize his or her own thoughts and views on a variety of topics, usually more related to his or her own life:
    - Which sports are better to play
    - Which groups are better to be included in
    - What personal appearances are desirable or attractive
    - What parental rules should be changed

Middle adolescence

With some experience in using more complex thinking processes, the focus of middle adolescence often expands to include more philosophical and futuristic concerns, including the following:

- Often questions more extensively
- Often analyzes more extensively
- Thinks about and begins to form his or her own code of ethics
- Thinks about different possibilities and begins to develop his or her own identity
- Thinks about and begins to systematically consider possible future goals
- Thinks about and begins to make his or her own plans
- Begins to think long-term
- Use of systematic thinking begins to influence relationships with others

Late adolescence

During late adolescence, complex thinking processes are used to focus on less self-centered concepts as well as personal decision making, including the following:

- Develops idealistic views on specific topics or concerns
- Debates and develops intolerance of opposing views
- Begins to focus thinking on making career decisions
- Begins to focus thinking on emerging role in adult society
- Increased thoughts about more global concepts, such as justice, history, politics, and patriotism

What encourages healthy cognitive development during adolescence?

The following suggestions will help to encourage positive and healthy cognitive development in the adolescent:

- Include adolescents in discussions about a variety of topics, issues, and current events.
- Encourage adolescents to share ideas and thoughts with adults.
- Encourage adolescents to think independently and to develop their own ideas.
- Assist adolescents in setting their own goals.
- Stimulate adolescents to think about possibilities of the future.
- Compliment and praise adolescents for well-thought-out decisions.
- Assist adolescents in re-evaluating poorly made decisions for themselves.

IDENTIFY MAJOR STAGES OF NORMAL MOTOR AND LANGUAGE DEVELOPMENT

The normal progression of learning demonstrated by a child is related to developmental growth in the areas of gross and fine motor abilities, as well as language development. This table presents a compilation of developmental milestones in motor and language skills that are normally achieved by children and youth of various ages.

Age	Motor (gross and fine)	Language (understood and spoken)
0-1 yrs.	• Sits without support • Develops one- and two-arm control crawls • Stands • Walks with aid • Begins to indicate	• Responds to sound (loud noises, mother's voice) • Turns to sources of sound • Babbles vowel and

	hand preference • Pincer grasp develops • Loses sight of object and searches • Transfers objects from one hand to another	consonant sounds • Responds with vocalization after adult speaks • Imitates sounds • Responds to words such as "up," "hello," "bye-bye," and "no" if adult gestures
1-2 yrs.	• Begins scribbling in repetitive, circular motions • Holds pencil or crayon in fist • Walks unaided • Steps up onto or down from low objects • Seats self • Turns pages several at a time • Throws small objects • Turns doorknobs	• Begins to express self with one word and increases to 50 words • Uses several suggestive words to describe events • Understands "bring it here," "take this to Daddy" • Uses "me" or "mine"
2-3 yrs.	• Begins a variety of scribbling patterns • Holds crayon or pencil with fingers and thumbs • Turns pages singly • Demonstrates stronger preference for one hand • Manipulates clay or dough • Runs forward well • Stands on one foot • Kicks • Walks on tiptoe	• Identifies pictures and objects when they are named • Joins words together in several phrases • Asks and answers questions • Enjoys listening to storybooks • Understands and uses "can't," "don't," "no" • Frustrated when spoken language is not

		• understood • Refers to self by name
3-4 yrs.	• Pounds nails or pegs successfully • Copies circles and attempts crosses such as "+" • Runs • Balances and hops on one foot • Pushes, pulls, steers toys • Pedals and steers tricycle • Throws balls overhead • Catches balls that are bounced • Jumps over, runs around objects	• Uses words in simple sentence form, such as "I see my book." • Adds "s" to indicate plural • Relates simple accounts of experiences • Carries out a sequence of simple directions • Begins to understand time concepts • Understands comparatives, such as bigger, smaller, closer • Language (understood and spoken) • Understands relationships indicated by "because" or "if"
4-5 yrs.	• Copies crossed lines or squares • Cuts on a line • Prints a few letters of alphabet • Walks backward • Jumps forward • Walks up and down stairs alternating feet • Draws human figures including head and "stick"	• Follows several unrelated commands • Listens to longer stories but often confuses them when re-telling • Asks "why," "how," "what for" questions • Understands comparatives, such as "fast,"

	arms and legs	• "faster," and "fastest" • Uses complex sentences such as "I like to play with my tricycle in and out of the house." • Uses relationship words, such as "because" or "so" • General speech is intelligible but may be frequently mispronounced
5-6 yrs.	• Runs on tiptoe • Walks on balance beam • Skips using alternate feet • Jumps rope • May ride two wheel bicycle • Roller skates • Copies triangles, name, numbers • Has firmly established handedness • Cuts and pastes large objects and designs • Includes more detail in drawing humans	• Generally communicates well with family and friends • Spoken language still has errors of subject-tense • Takes turns in conversation • Receives and gives information • With exceptions, use of grammar matches that of adults in family and neighborhood
7-10 yrs.	• Continued development and refinement of small muscles in writing, drawing, handling	• Develops ability to understand that words and pictures are representational

	tools • Masters physical skills for game playing • Physical skills become important with peers and self-concept	of real objects • Understands most vocabulary used • Begins to use language aggressively • Verbalizes similarities and differences • Uses language to exchange ideas • Uses abstract words, slang, and often profanity
11-15 yrs.	• Adolescent growth spurts begin • May experience uneven growth resulting in awkwardness or clumsiness • Continued improvement in motor development and coordination	• Has good command of spoken and written language • Uses language extensively to discuss feelings and other more abstract ideas • Uses abstract words discriminately and selectively • Uses written language extensively

SOURCE: Gearhart, B. R. 1985. Learning disabilities: Educational strategies, (4th ed.), Appendix B: 371-373. Printed with permission of Charles E. Merrill.

Skill 1.2 **Demonstrating knowledge of the types, etiology, identification criteria, characteristics, and continuum of severity of various disabilities**

A table summarizing the classification of students with disabilities and the characteristics of each major classification is found at the end of this skill set. That classification system is used to help define both eligibility for special services and placement in special service programs. Many of the classifications are medical or physical in nature and the terminology is self-explanatory (e.g., blindness). Other categories, particularly "Specific Learning Disability," include a wide range of disabilities and it is important for the teacher to understand the terminology of these disabilities when applied to his or her students. Listed below are some of the most common *specific learning disabilities* teachers will encounter in their students with special needs:

- **Central Auditory Processing Deficit (CAPD):** Students with CAPDs have normal hearing *physiologically*, but have deficits in the processing or auditory input. Such deficits impact both cognitive and linguistic functioning in both receptive and expressive modes. The symptoms sometimes are mistaken for ADHD, because the child cannot adequately process instructions and information.
- **Communication Disorders:** This group includes deficits in language processing, articulation, fluency, or voice.
- **Dyscalculia:** Any serious disability in processing mathematical information, concepts or calculations, particularly when there are *not* corresponding disabilities in other verbal skills.
- **Dysgraphia:** A serious deficit in the ability to carry out the motor or cognitive functions necessary to be able to write. This may be a motor problem and/or a cognitive inability to plan and generate sentences. It is usually neurologically based.
- **Dyslexia:** Although this term is not as widely used as it once was, it still refers to a reading disability that is based in problems learning to associate sounds and symbols (letters).
- **Nonverbal Learning Disabilities:** These disabilities impact many areas of nonverbal problem solving. Although children with them can often "read" and memorize well, they have significant difficulty understanding what they read, as well as difficulty understanding nonverbal communication such as facial expressions and body language. As a result, both social competence and emotional well-being can be impacted. There may also be deficits in visual-spatial organization and motor control.
- **Pervasive Developmental Disorders Not Otherwise Specified (PDDNOS):** These disorders are very similar to autism and are sometimes referred to as "autism spectrum disorders." Though children with these disorders do not qualify as autistic, they have many of the same deficits in social and communication skills.

In addition to specific learning disabilities, special education teachers may often encounter the following diagnoses of children with special needs:

- **Attention Deficit Disorder (ADD) or Attention Deficit with Hyperactivity Disorder (ADHD):** Children with these disorders display serious inattention, distractibility, disorganization, and poor impulse control, often with constant movement or activity they cannot control. Typically, they do not show delayed cognition or mental retardation. These disorders can often accompany other medical or learning disorders, however, and can further impact learning.
- **Asperger's Syndrome:** Although the definition of this disorder is changing in some quarters, it usually refers to a type of autism involving most of the characteristics of autism, without cognitive delay or retardation. Children with this disorder have normal or above average cognitive abilities. It is often referred to as a "high functioning form of autism."
- **Cerebral Palsy:** This is a neurological disorder that involves damage to the motor centers of the brain (during fetal development, or during or after birth) and results in tremors, muscle weakness or tension. Both gross and fine motor skills can be affected.
- **Developmental Disabilities:** These disabilities result in significant delays in physical (e.g., Cerebral Palsy) or cognitive (mental retardation) abilities.
- **Tourette Syndrome:** This is a seizure disorder (not epilepsy) that produces motor, vocal, and other tics (i.e., highly repetitive actions) over which the child has minimum control.

BEHAVIORAL ISSUES

In order to tackle the issue of behavior problems, educators usually start with a *Behavior Intervention Plan* (BIP). One of the first steps to developing a BIP entails taking a detailed *Functional Behavior Assessment* (FBA) summary, which must define behaviors in observable and measurable terms along four variables: *Frequency, Duration, Intensity*, and *Degree of Severity*.

The FBA must note the frequency of the behaviors that have been identified. Frequency consists of how often a behavior occurs in a specified time block. (e.g., morning, afternoon, evening). The activity during which the behavior typically occurs is also recorded. For example, does it occur during lunch, transitions, group time, or another time period? The data should indicate the frequency of the individual behaviors and note when it is less frequent or when the behavior is most likely to occur.

The FBA can help identify the following:

- When the behavior was first observed and key events at that time
- Any signs or cues from the student that help predict that the behavior will occur

- What happens just before the behavior that may trigger the behavior
- Settings, situations, and other variables that influence the behavior

These observations should include the following:

- Specific days or times of day
- Specific settings such as school, home, class, hallway, or bus
- Particular subject areas such as math or P.E.
- Type or length of assignment
- The manner of presenting instruction, feedback, or corrections
- The particular person presenting the information

Another variable that must be addressed is the duration of the behaviors. This variable entails measuring how long the behavior takes place by timing the behavior from start to finish and writing it down.

A third variable that must be measured is the intensity of the behavior. The FBA must have a scale that assesses whether the behavior is of low, medium, or high intensity. If the student is having a tantrum, is there a scale to measure the intensity of the tantrum? For example, a highly intense tantrum might include hitting the teacher or classmates, while a less intense tantrum may include property damage.

A fourth variable that is measured when assessing behavior is the degree of severity. All behaviors can be put into different categories, depending on their impact. More severe behavior problems would involve physical violence and destruction of property, while less severe problems will involve screaming, yelling, and general disruption of class time.

The FBA may also include factors such as:

- When, where, and with whom the behavior is least likely to occur
- Specific skill deficits that interfere with the student's ability to behave as expected
- Whether the student is aware of expected behavior and understands the consequences of the behavior
- Whether the student has the skills necessary to behave as expected
- The apparent function of undesirable behavior (what the student gets, avoids, or escapes due to the behavior)
- Potential reinforcers for the student

Classification

The classification of student exceptionalities and disabilities in education is a categorical system; it organizes special education into categories. Within the categories are subdivisions that may be based on the severity or level of support services needed. Having a categorical system allows educators to differentiate and define types of disabilities, relate treatments to certain categories, and concentrate research and advocacy efforts. The disadvantage of the categorical system is the labeling of groups or individuals. Critics of labels say that labeling can place the emphasis on the label and not the individual needs of the child.

The following table summarizes the categories of disabilities and major characteristics of their definitions under IDEA.

Classification	Characteristics
Autism*	Impairment in social interaction and communication, accompanied by restricted repetitive and stereotyped patterns of behavior, interests, and activities, occurring before age 3.
Deaf	Impairment in processing linguistic information, with or without hearing aids, that has an adverse impact on educational performance.
Deaf-blind	Hearing and visual impairments causing communication, developmental, and education problems too severe to be met in programs solely for deaf or blind children
Hard of Hearing	Permanent or fluctuating hearing impairment that adversely affects educational performance but is not included in the definition of deafness
Mentally Retarded	Significantly subaverage general intellectual functioning with deficits in adaptive behavior, manifested during the developmental period, and adversely affecting educational performance
Multihandicapped	Combination of impairments, excluding deaf-blind children, that cause educational problems too severe to be serviced in programs designed for a single impairment
Orthopedically Impaired	Severe orthopedic impairment resulting from birth defects, disease (e.g., polio), or other causes (e.g., amputation, burns) that adversely affects

Classification	Characteristics
	educational performance
Other Health Impaired	Medical conditions such as heart conditions, tuberculosis, rheumatic fever, nephritis, asthma, sickle cell anemia, hemophilia, epilepsy, lead poisoning, leukemia, or diabetes. (IDEA listing). Other health conditions may be included if they are so chronic or acute that the child's strength, vitality, or alertness is limited.
Seriously Emotionally Disturbed (Does not include children who are socially maladjusted unless they are also classified as seriously emotionally disturbed.)	Schizophrenia, and conditions in which one or more of these characteristics is exhibited over a long period of time and to a marked degree: a) inability to learn not explained by intellectual, sensory, or health factors, b) inability to build or maintain satisfactory interpersonal relationships, c) inappropriate types of behavior or feelings, d) general pervasive unhappiness or depression, e) tendency to develop physical symptoms or fears associated with personal or school problems.
Specific Learning Disability	Disorder in one or more basic psychological processes involved in understanding or in using spoken or written language, which manifests itself in an imperfect ability to listen, think, speak, read, write, spell, or to do mathematical calculations. Disorders cannot be attributed to visual, hearing, physical, intellectual, or emotional handicaps, or cultural, environmental, or economic disadvantage.
Speech Impaired	Communication disorder such as stuttering, impaired articulation, voice impairment, or language impairment adversely affecting educational performance.
Visually Handicapped	Visual impairment, even with correction,

Classification	Characteristics
(Partially sighted or blind)	adversely affecting educational performance

*Autism was added as a separate category of disability in 1990 under P. L. 101-476. This addition was not a change in the law but a clarification. The law previously covered students with autism, but now the law identifies them as a separate and distinct class entitled to the law's benefits. Autism is a developmental disability significantly affecting verbal and nonverbal communication and social interaction, generally evident before age 3, which adversely affects a child's educational performance. Other characteristics often associated with autism are engagement in repetitive activities and stereotyped movements, resistance to environmental change or change in daily routines, and unusual responses to sensory experiences. The term does not apply if a child's educational performance is adversely affected primarily because the child has a serious emotional disturbance. It should also be noted that there is no classification for gifted children under IDEA. Funding and services for gifted programs are left up to the individual states and school districts. Therefore, the number of districts providing services and the scope of gifted programs varies among states and school districts.

Skill 1.3 Demonstrating familiarity with similarities and differences among individuals with disabilities, including those with coexisting disabilities

Children who have multiple disabilities are an extremely heterogeneous population. Their characteristics are determined by the type and severity of their combined disabilities; therefore, they differ in their sensory, motor, social, and cognitive abilities. Although any number of combinations of disabilities is possible, major dimensions typically include mental retardation, neurological impairments, emotional disturbance, or deafness and blindness. Those whose impairments combine to form multiple disabilities often exhibit characteristics on a severe level. Low self-esteem and poor social skills often characterize this population. Youngsters with severe disabilities may possess profound language or perceptual-cognitive deprivations. Moreover, they may have extremely fragile physiological conditions. Children with severe disabilities are classified by the extent of the disabilities.

Among the characteristics that can be present in students with severe or profound multidisabilities are:

- Often not toilet trained
- Frequently nonambulatory
- Aggressiveness toward others without provocation, and antisocial behavior
- Markedly withdrawn or unresponsive to others
- No attention to even the most pronounced social stimuli
- Self-mutilation (head banging, biting, and scratching or cutting of self)

- Rumination (self-induced vomiting, swallowing vomit)
- Self-stimulation (rocking, hand-flapping)
- Intense temper tantrums of unknown origin
- Excessive, pointless imitation, or the total absence of the ability to imitate
- Inability to be controlled verbally
- Extremely brittle medical existence (life-threatening conditions such as congenital heart disease, respiratory difficulties, metabolic disorders, central nervous system disorders, and digestive malfunctions)

Seldom does a student with a disability fall into only one of the categories listed in IDEA 2004. For example, a student with a hearing impairment might also have a specific learning disability, or a student on the autism spectrum might also demonstrate language impairment. In fact, language impairment is inherent in autism. Sometimes the eligibility is defined as multiple disabilities (with one listed as a primary eligibility on the IEP and the others listed as secondary). Sometimes there are overlapping needs that are not necessarily listed as a secondary disability.

Teachers of special education students should be aware of the similarities between areas of disabilities, as well as the differences.

Students with disabilities (in all areas) may demonstrate difficulties with social skills. For a student with a hearing impairment, social skills may be difficult because the student does not hear conversations. An autistic student might be unaware of the social cues given with voice, facial expression, and body language. Both of these students need social skill instruction, but each in a different way.

Students with disabilities in all areas may demonstrate difficulties in academic performance. A student with mental retardation will need special instruction across all areas of academics, while a student with a learning disability may need assistance in only one or two subject areas.

Students with disabilities may demonstrate difficulties with independence or self-help skills. A student with a visual impairment may need specific mobility training, while a student with a specific learning disability may need a checklist to help manage materials and assignments.

Special education teachers should be aware that although students across disabilities might demonstrate difficulties in similar ways, the causes could be very different and the treatment will be different as well.

Additionally, special education teachers should be aware that each area of disability has a range of involvement. Some students might have minimal disability and require no services. Others might need only a few accommodations and have a 504 plan. Some might need an IEP that outlines a specific special education program that could be implemented in an inclusion/resource program, in a self-contained program, or in a residential setting. For example, a student with ADD might be able to participate in the regular education program with a 504 plan that outlines a checklist system to keep the student organized and with additional communication between school and home. Other students with ADD might need instruction in a smaller group with fewer distractions; they might be better served in a resource room.

Because of the unique needs of each child, such programs are documented in the child's IEP (individualized education plan).

COMPETENCY 002   UNDERSTAND FACTORS THAT AFFECT DEVELOPMENT AND LEARNING IN STUDENTS WITH DISABILITIES

Skill 2.1   Recognizing the educational implications of various types of disabilities, including coexisting disabilities

See Skill 1.2.

Skill 2.2   Demonstrating knowledge of the roles families play in supporting students' development and learning

The needs of the whole child must be considered in order to understand the child's learning style, temperament, and requirements. Therefore, information should be gathered from various sources.

Besides the general education teacher, a vital person or persons in the assessment process should be the parent(s). The parent(s) can provide needed background information on the child, such as a brief medical, physical, and developmental history. Paraprofessionals, doctors, and other professionals are also very helpful in providing necessary information about the child, but the family is a direct, primary source of pertinent information.

The following are ways of gathering information:

- **Interview:** Interviews can be in person or on paper. The related parties can be invited to a meeting to conduct the interview; if the parent does not respond after several attempts, the paper interview may be sent or mailed home.
- **Questionnaires:** Questionnaires are also a good way of gathering information.
  Some questionnaires may have open-ended questions, and some may have several questions that are to be answered using a rating scale. The answerer is to circle ratings ranging from 1 to 5, or 1 to 7 (Strongly Disagree to Strongly Agree).
- **Conference/meeting:** With parents' permission, it may be useful to conduct a meeting—either one-on-one or in a group setting—to gather information about the child. Everyone who may be able to offer any information about the child and his or her academic progress, physical development, social skills, behavior, medical history, and/or needs should be invited to attend.

Relevant background information regarding the student's academic, medical, and family histories should be used to identify students with disabilities and evaluate their progress. It is also critical for collaborating with both families and the students themselves. Refer to the student's IEP as a document that provides further information previously stated by family members.

The IEP and supplemental evaluations should include:

- Developmental history
- Relevant medical history—including the presence or absence of a medical diagnosis for the present symptoms
- Academic history—including results of prior standardized testing
- Reports of classroom performance
- Relevant family history— including the primary language of the home and the student's (and parents') current level of fluency of English
- Relevant psychosocial history
- Discussion of dual diagnosis, alternative or co-existing mood, behavioral, neurological, and/or personality disorders, along with any history of relevant medication use that may affect the individual's learning
- Exploration of possible alternatives that could mimic a learning disability

By utilizing all possible background information in the assessment, the team can rule out alternative explanations for academic problems, such as poor education, poor motivation and study skills, emotional problems, or cultural and language differences. If the student's entire background and history is not taken into account, it is not always possible to institute the most appropriate educational program for the student with disabilities.

Skill 2.3 Demonstrating knowledge of the lifelong impact of disabilities on students and their families

Although legal and educational definitions of the various disabilities state that they may NOT be due to cultural diversity or socio-economic environment, these factors do impact children with disabilities in special ways. Quite often, students absorb the familial, cultural, and social environment around them without deciphering the contextual meaning of the experiences. When provided with a diversity of cultural contexts, some students with exceptionalities cannot adapt and incorporate multiple meanings from cultural cues vastly different from their own backgrounds.

Sociocultural and family-related factors have a definitive impact on students' psychological, emotional, affective, and physiological development, and on academic learning and future opportunities.

The educational experience for most students is a complex experience with a diversity of interlocking meanings and inferences. If one aspect of the complexity is altered, it affects other aspects, which may have an impact on how a student or teacher views an instructional or learning experience. With the current demographic profile of today's school communities, the complexity of understanding, interpreting, and synthesizing nuances from the diversity of familial and cultural lineages can provide many communication and learning impediments that could hamper the acquisition of learning, especially for students with exceptionalities.

Teachers must create personalized learning communities where every student is a valued member of and contributor to the classroom experiences. In classrooms where sociocultural attributes of the student population are incorporated into the fabric of the learning process, dynamic interrelationships are created that enhance the learning experience and the personalization of learning. When students with exceptionalities are provided with numerous academic and social opportunities to share cultural approaches to learning, everyone in the classroom benefits from bonding through shared experiences and an expanded viewpoint of a world experience that vastly differs from their own.

Similarly, *inclusion of students with exceptionalities into the general education classroom can be beneficial for advanced academic achievement as well as sociocultural development*, provided proper accommodations for their special needs are made. Researchers continue to show that personalized learning environments increase learning for students, decrease drop-out rates among marginalized students, and decrease unproductive student behavior that can result from constant cultural misunderstandings or miscues among students.

Learning environments can help children with and without disabilities understand that, though learning abilities and styles differ, each child has a place in and something to contribute to the group. This approach can prevent misunderstandings and intolerance of students with special needs. *Promoting diversity of learning and cultural competency in the classroom creates a world of multicultural opportunities and learning.* When students are able to step outside their comfort zones and share the world of a homeless student or empathize with an English Language Learner (ELL) who has just immigrated to the United States, is learning English for the first time, and is still trying to keep up with the academic learning in an unfamiliar language, then students grow exponentially in social understanding and cultural connectedness.

Personalized learning communities provide supportive learning environments that address the academic and emotional needs of all students. As sociocultural knowledge is conveyed continuously in the interrelated experiences shared cooperatively and collaboratively in student groupings and in individualized learning, the current and future benefits will continue to present the case and importance of understanding the whole child, inclusive of the social and cultural context.

Skill 2.4   Recognizing ways in which teacher attitudes, behaviors, and cultural competence affect individuals with disabilities

Just as cultures place varying values on education and gender roles, they also hold different views of individuals with disabilities, including appropriate education, career goals, and the individual's role in society. *The special educator must first become familiar with the cultural backgrounds of the students and of the community in which he or she teaches.* When the special educator demonstrates respect for each individual student's culture, he or she will build the rapport necessary to work with the student, family, and community to prepare the student for future productive work, independence, and possible post-secondary education or training (IDEA 2004).

Also see Skill 7.1.

INFLUENCE OF TEACHER ATTITUDES

The attitude of the teacher can have both a positive and negative impact on student performance. *A teacher's attitude is the expectation that the teacher may have toward the student's potential performance, as well as how the teacher behaves toward the student. This attitude can impact the student's self-image as well as his or her academic performance.*

Negative teacher attitudes toward students with disabilities are detrimental to the handicapped students mainstreamed in general education classrooms. The phenomenon of a self-fulfilling prophecy is based on the attitude of the teacher. In the context of education, this means that the predictions of a teacher about the ability of a student to achieve or not to achieve educational objectives are often proven to be correct.

This phenomenon also occurs in more subtle ways. Even without realizing it, teachers communicate their expectations of individual students. In turn, the students may adjust their behaviors to match the teacher's expectations. Based on this, the teacher's expectations of what will happen come true.

Researchers in psychology and education have investigated this occurrence and have discovered that many people are sensitive to verbal and nonverbal cues from others regarding how they expect to be treated. As a result, they may consciously and subconsciously change their behaviors and attitudes to conform to another person's hopes. Depending on the expectation, this can be either advantageous or detrimental.

The teacher's attitude toward a student can be shaped by a number of variables, including race, ethnicity, disability, behavior, appearance, and social class. All of these variables can impact the teacher's attitude toward the student and how the student will achieve academically.

Teachers have the responsibility to not allow their negative attitudes toward students to impact how they perceive the students interact with them. If the teacher is able to communicate to all of his or her students that they all have great potential, and if he or she is optimistic regarding this, then the students should excel in some aspect of their educational endeavors. This continues to be true for as long as the teacher is able to make the student believe in him or herself.

It can be hard for teachers to maintain a positive attitude at all times with all students. However, it is important to be encouraging to all students at all times, because every student has the potential to be successful in school. Consistent encouragement can help turn a C student into a B or even an A student. At the same time, negative feedback can lead to failure and loss of self-esteem.

Teachers should utilize their verbal communication skills to ensure that the things they communicate to students are said in the most positive manner possible. For example, instead of saying, "You talk too much," it would be more positive to state, "You have excellent verbal communication skills and are very sociable."

Teachers have a major influence on what happens in their classrooms, because they are the primary decision makers. They set the tone for how the information they distribute is absorbed.

In order for teachers to rise above their prejudices and preset attitudes, it is important that teachers are given training and support services to enable them to deal with students who come from challenging backgrounds or present challenging behaviors.

Skill 2.5   **Demonstrating familiarity with the general effects of various types of medications (e.g., anti-seizure, stimulant, antidepressant) on the educational, cognitive, physical, social, and emotional behavior of individuals with disabilities**

Students with disabilities who take medications often experience medication side effects that can impact their behaviors and educational development. Some medications may impair concentration, which can lead to poor processing ability, lower alertness, and cause drowsiness or hyperactivity. Students who take several medications often have an increased risk of behavioral and cognitive side effects.

The student's parents should inform the school when their child is beginning or changing his or her medication so teachers and staff can look out for possible side effects. It is important for both the teacher and the school nurse to maintain close communication with the child's parents and report any behaviors (positive or negative) that may result from the medication.

ANTIDEPRESSANTS

There are three different classes of antidepressants that students may take. One type is called *selective serotonin-reuptake inhibitors* (SSRIs). The SSRIs block certain receptors in the brain from absorbing the chemical serotonin. Over time, SSRIs may cause changes in brain chemistry. The side effects of SSRIs include dry mouth, insomnia or restless sleep, increased sweating, and nausea. They can also cause mood swings in students with bipolar disorders.

A second type is *tricyclic antidepressants*. They are often effective for treating depression and obsessive-compulsive behavior. They cause side effects similar to the SSRIs, such as sedation, tremors, seizures, dry mouth, light sensitivity, and mood swings in students with bipolar disorders.

A third type of antidepressant is *monoamine oxidase inhibitors* (MAOIs). These are not as widely used as the other two types, because many have unpleasant and life-threatening interactions with many other drugs, including common over-the-counter medications. Students taking MAOIs must also follow a special diet because these medications interact with many foods. The list of foods to avoid includes chocolate, aged cheeses, and more.

STIMULANTS

Stimulants are often prescribed to help students with attention deficit disorder and attention deficit hyperactivity disorder. These drugs can have many side effects, including agitation, restlessness, aggressive behavior, dizziness, insomnia, headache, or tremors. Nonstimulant medications can also be used to treat these disorders when stimulants are not appropriate for the child.

TRANQUILIZERS

For severe cases of anxiety, an anti-anxiety medication (tranquilizer) may be prescribed. Most tranquilizers have a potential for addiction and abuse. They tend to be sedating and can cause a variety of unpleasant side effects, including blurred vision, confusion, sleepiness, and tremors.

WHAT EDUCATORS SHOULD KNOW

If educators are aware of the types of medication that their students are taking, along with the myriad of side effects, they will be able to respond more positively when some of the side effects of the medication change their students' behaviors, response rates, and attention spans.

Medical complications must be considered when developing schedules and curricular plans. Students may miss school due to medical conditions that require extensive rest or hospital-based intervention. Cooperative programs with home and hospital teachers can decrease the impact of such absences.

Also of considerable concern is the tendency to overcompensate. Teachers should try not to focus too much on the medical implications of a student's handicap. Interruptions for suctioning, administering medication, or other medical interventions should not be disruptive to the classroom and learning atmosphere. *Focus should be on maximizing opportunities for educational success and social interaction, not on limitations and isolation.* For example, class parties can include food treats that meet a student's dietary restrictions, or medical intervention can be completed during individual work times rather than during group learning activity periods.

Students with seizures will require considerable medical support. A seizure is an abnormal electrical discharge in the brain. Incidences and behaviors range from experiencing odd tastes or smells to jerking and spasms throughout the body. The individual may experience altered consciousness or the loss of consciousness, muscle control, or bladder control. Seizures may be triggered by repetitive sounds, flashing lights, video games, touching certain parts of the body, certain drugs, low sugar level, or low oxygen levels in the blood.

Asthma is another well-known condition found in students with and without disabilities. Asthma is a condition in which the person's airway becomes inflamed. The inflammation may cause coughing, wheezing, tightness of chest, and shortness of breath. The cause of asthma is not completely known, but research indicates that if children are exposed to tobacco smoke, infections, and some allergens early in life, it will increase their chances of developing asthma. Research also indicates that there may be a genetic connection; in many cases, children who have asthma have other family members with this condition. Short-acting inhaled beta-agonists are the preferred quick-relief medicine. The most common side effects of beta-agonists inhalers are rapid heartbeat, headache, nervousness, and trembling.

Juvenile diabetes (type 1) is another condition that may affect students. Those with juvenile diabetes are typically under the age of 30. It is a condition in which the pancreas cannot produce insulin, or insulin is produced in extremely small amounts. People with type 1 diabetes need to take insulin injections in order to live. A student with diabetes should be allowed to eat snacks during the day, monitor his or her blood-sugar level, and take insulin shots.

Some students may also require tube feeding. Tube feeding is a method of providing nutrition to people who cannot sufficiently obtain calories by eating or to those who cannot eat because they have difficulty swallowing. Tubes that transport nutritional formulas can be inserted into the stomach (G tubes), through the nose and into the stomach (NG tubes), or through the nose and into the small intestine (NJ tubes). The NG and NJ tubes are considered to be temporary; the G tube is considered more permanent, but it can be removed. Tube feeding is common among students with dysphagia, a condition that hampers swallowing.

DOMAIN II	ASSESSING STUDENTS AND DEVELOPING PROGRAMS
COMPETENCY 003	UNDERSTAND PROCEDURES FOR SELECTING AND ADMINISTERING VARIOUS TYPES OF ASSESSMENTS TO ADDRESS THE INDIVIDUAL NEEDS OF STUDENTS WITH DISABILITIES.
Skill 3.1	Recognizing the uses and limitations of various formal and informal assessments (e.g., statewide achievement tests, intelligence tests, observations, behavior rating scales, inventories)

Assessment is the gathering of information in order to make decisions. In education, assessments typically focus on student performance, progress, and behavior.

PURPOSES OF ASSESSMENT

In the education of students with exceptionalities, assessment is used to make decisions about the following:

- Screening and initial identification of children who may need services
- Diagnosis of specific learning disabilities
- Selection and evaluation of teaching strategies and programs
- Determination of the child's present level of performance in academics
- Classification and program placement
- Development of goals, objectives, and evaluation for the IEP
- Eligibility for a program
- Continuation of a program
- Effectiveness of instructional programs and strategies
- Effectiveness of behavioral interventions
- Accommodations needed for mandated or classroom testing

TYPES OF ASSESSMENT

Assessment types can be categorized in a number of ways, most commonly in terms of what is being assessed, how the assessment is constructed, or how it is to be used. It is important to understand these differences in order to be able to correctly interpret assessment results.

Formal vs. Informal

This variable focuses on how the assessment is constructed or scored. *Formal assessments* are assessments such as standardized tests or textbook quizzes; objective tests that include primarily questions for which there is only one correct, easily identifiable answer. These can be commercial or teacher-made assessments, given to either groups or individuals. *Informal assessments* have fewer objective measures, and may include anecdotes or observations that may or may not be quantified, interviews, informal questioning during a task, etc. An example might be watching a student sort objects to see what attribute is most important to the student, or questioning a student to see what he or she found confusing about a task.

Standardized Tests

Standardized tests are formal tests that are administered to either groups or individuals in a specifically prescribed manner, with strict rules to keep procedures, scoring, and interpretation of results uniform in all cases. Such tests allow comparisons to be made across populations, ages, or grades, or over time for a particular student. Intelligence tests and most diagnostic tests are standardized tests.

Norm Referenced vs. Criterion Referenced

This distinction is based on the standard to which the student's performance is being compared. *Norm referenced* tests establish a ranking and compare the student's performance to an established norm, usually for age or grade peers. What the student knows is of less importance than how similar the student's performance is to a specific group. Norm referenced tests are, by definition, standardized. Examples include intelligence tests and many achievement tests. Norm referenced tests are often used in determining eligibility for special needs services. *Criterion Referenced* tests measure a student's knowledge of specific content, usually related to classroom instruction. The student's performance is compared to a set of criteria or a pre-established standard of information the student is expected to know. On these tests, what the student knows is more important than how he or she compares to other students. Examples include math quizzes at the end of a chapter, or some state-mandated tests of specific content. Criterion referenced tests are used to determine whether a student has mastered required skills.

Group vs. Individual Assessments

This variable simply refers to the manner of presentation; whether the assessment is administered to a group of students or on a one-to-one basis. Group assessments can be formal or informal, standardized or not, criterion or norm referenced. Individual assessments can be found in all these types as well.

Authentic Assessments

Authentic assessments are designed to be as close to real life as possible so that they are relevant and meaningful to the student's life. They can be formal or informal, depending upon how they are constructed. An example of an authentic test item would be to ask students to calculate a 20 percent sales discount on a popular clothing item, after the students have studied math percentages.

Rating Scales and Checklists

Rating scales and checklists are generally self-appraisal instruments completed by the student or observation-based instruments completed by teacher or parents. The focus is frequently on behavior or affective areas such as interest, motivation, attention or depression. These tests can be formal or informal and some can be standardized and norm referenced. Examples of norm referenced tests of this type would be ADHD rating scales or the Behavior Assessment System for Children.

Screening, Diagnosis, and Placement

Intelligence tests have historically been considered relatively good predictors of school performance. These tests are standardized and norm referenced. Examples are the *Wechsler Intelligence Scale for Children-Fourth Edition (WISC-IV), Stanford-Binet IV*, and *Kaufman Assessment Battery for Children-Second Edition (KACB-II)*. Some intelligence tests are designed for use with groups and are used for screening and identification purposes. The individual tests are used for classification and program placement. Since intelligence is a quality that is difficult to define precisely, results of intelligence tests should not be used to discriminate or define the person's potential. In recent years intelligence testing has evolved to include measures of multiple intelligences (Gardner, 1999) and these tests can further refine placement decisions for students with special needs. In many cases a significant discrepancy between scores on different intelligences helps to identify specific learning disabilities. Such measures also help show how a disability impacts performance in different areas of the curriculum.

There are many standardized achievement and educational skills tests, including state mandated testing, that are also used by school systems to help determine eligibility and placement.

Skill 3.2 Demonstrating knowledge of screening, prereferral, referral, and eligibility procedures (e.g., to address a student's academic functioning and/or mental health needs)

ELIGIBILITY

Eligibility is based on criteria defined in federal law or state regulations, which vary from state to state. Evaluation methods correspond with eligibility criteria for the special education classifications. For example, a multidisciplinary evaluation for a student being evaluated for intellectual disabilities would include the individual's intellectual functioning, adaptive behavior, and achievement levels. Other tests are based on developmental characteristics exhibited (e.g., social, language, and motor).

A student evaluated for learning disabilities is given reading, math, and spelling achievement tests, an intelligence test to confirm average or above average cognitive capabilities, and tests of written and oral language ability. Tests need to show a discrepancy between potential and performance. Classroom observations and samples of student work (such as impaired reading ability or impaired writing ability) also provide indicators of possible learning disabilities.

Eligibility for services in behavior disorders requires documented evidence of social deficiencies or learning deficits that are not because of intellectual, sensory, or physical conditions. Therefore, any student undergoing multidisciplinary evaluation for this categorical service is usually given an intelligence test, diagnostic achievement tests, and social and/or adaptive inventories. Results of behavior frequency lists, direct observations, and anecdotal records collected over an extended period often accompany test results.

Additional information frequently used when making decisions about a child's eligibility for special education include the following:

- Developmental history
- Past academic performance
- Medical history or records
- Neurological reports
- Classroom observations
- Speech and language evaluations
- Personality assessment
- Discipline reports
- Home visits
- Parent interviews
- Samples of student work

If considered eligible for special education services, the child's disability should be documented in a written report stating specific reasons for the decision.

Three-year reevaluations (*Triennials*) of a student's progress are required by law and determine the growth and changing needs of the student. During the reevaluation, continued eligibility for services in special education must be assessed using a range of evaluation tools similar to those used during the initial evaluation. All relevant information about the student is considered when making a decision about whether the student's eligibility should be continued. If the student no longer needs the service and is deemed ready to exit the program, then planning for the transition must occur.

INDIVIDUAL EDUCATION PLAN

Before placement can occur, the multidisciplinary team must develop an *Individualized Education Plan* (IEP), a child-centered educational plan that is tailored to meet individual needs. IEPs acknowledge each student's requirements for a specially designed educational program.

The following three purposes are identified by Polloway, Patton, Payne, and Payne (1989):

1. IEPs outline instructional programs. They provide specific instructional direction, which eliminates any pulling together of marginally related instructional exercises.
2. IEPs function as the basis for evaluation.
3. IEPs facilitate communication among staff members, teachers, and parents, and to some extent, teachers, and students.

Development of the IEP follows initial identification, evaluation, and classification. The educational plan is evaluated and rewritten at least annually. An IEP is a binding legal document, and both the school system and the teacher are responsible for seeing that its conditions are met. An IEP also follows the child from school to school when the child moves.

PLACEMENT

The law defines Special Education and identifies related services that may be required if Special Education is to be effective. By law, a Special Education delivery service placement must be in the student's least restrictive environment. Special Education services occur at a variety of levels, some more restrictive than others. The largest number of students (those with mild disabilities) is served in settings closest to normal educational placements. Service delivery in more restrictive settings is limited to students with severe or profound disabilities, who compose a smaller population within special education. The exception is correctional facilities, which serve a limited and restricted populace.

One way to organize the options for placement of special education students is shown on the *Cascade System of Special Education Services (Deno, 1970), (see also Skill 5.1).* The multidisciplinary team must be able to match the needs of the student with an appropriate placement in the cascade system of services. According to Polloway, et al. (1994), two assumptions are made when we use the cascade of services as a guide to place students. First, a child should be placed in an educational setting as close to the regular classroom as possible, and placed only as far away from this least restrictive environment as necessary to provide an appropriate education.

Second, program exit should be a goal. A student's placement may change when the team obtains data suggesting the advisability of an alternative educational setting. As adaptive, social, cognitive, motor, and language skills are developed, the student may be placed in a less restrictive environment. The multidisciplinary team is responsible for monitoring and recommending placement changes when appropriate.

BEHAVIORAL AND EMOTIONAL ASSESSMENT

Standardized measures of behavior involve direct observation with a behavior rating scale. Measurement of emotional state involves inference and subjectivity on the part of the examiner.

Behavior Rating Scales

Examples of these scales are the *Revised Behavior Problem Checklist*, *Behavior Rating Profile*, and *Burks Behavior Rating Scales*. Items may be grouped according to categorical characteristics. For the *Revised Behavior Problem Checklist*, the four major scales are Conduct Disorder, Socialized Aggression, Attention Problem-Immaturity, and Anxiety-Withdrawn, with minor scales of Psychotic Behavior and Motor Excess.

Behavior-rating scales require that the examiner rate examples of behaviors on Likert-type scales, such as 0 = not a problem, 1 = mild problem, and 2 = severe problem. Each scale has its own set of scoring procedures. Therefore, the teacher must be sure to consult the test manual before attempting to interpret the results. The following are other factors to consider when interpreting behavior-rating scales:

- **Reliability and validity information:** norm group information and relevant research on the test instrument
- **Sources of information:** some tests include parent and youth reports or measure behavior across a number of settings in and out of school.
- **Suggested uses of the results:** some tests are intended for screening but not diagnostic purposes.
- **Scoring and profile information:** for example, the *Child Behavior Checklist and Revised Behavior Profile* lists three social-competency scales and behavior problem scales identified by factor analysis for boys and girls in three separate age ranges.

Measures of Emotional State

These tests are designed to be administered by trained psychologists and psychiatrists. The child's emotional state is inferred by analyzing observable behavior. Types of tests include projective methods, measures of self-concept, and inventories and questionnaires.

Projective methods

The theory behind these methods is that a person will project his or her own meaning, patterns, feelings, and significance onto ambiguous stimuli. Because these tests are subjective, it is difficult to establish reliability and validity; therefore, their usefulness for educational purposes is limited. Some examples of these tests are:

- *Rorschach Ink Blot Test:* the individual states what he "sees" in each of ten inkblots. Diagnostic interpretation is based on clinical data.
- *Thematic Apperception Test:* the examiner uses a series of 31 pictures and asks the child to tell a story about them. The examiner looks for themes in the stories, especially those relating to the main character.

When interpreting these tests attention must be paid to the following: the reliability and validity, the training of the examiner, and the subjective quality.

Self-concept measures

Some familiar examples are the *Tennessee Self-Concept Scale* and *Piers-Harris Children's Self-Concept scale*. Most instruments use a system of self-evaluation and self-report. Therefore, the child might choose the answer that he or she believes the examiner wants to see. In addition, because self-concept is a difficult construct to define, there is the problem of adequate validity.

Inventories and questionnaires

Many of these are designed for measuring the emotional and personality characteristics of adolescents and adults. These tests are often self-reported, although some, such as the *Personality Inventory for Children (PIC)*, include a parent report. Results are grouped into such scales as adjustment, achievement, depression, delinquency, and anxiety. These results are generally used with classification and placement decisions. Reliability and validity should be considered when interpreting these tests.

The *PIC* was designed specifically for evaluating children. The parent completes the true/false items, and three validity scales are included to determine the *truthfulness* of the responses. Thirteen of the thirty scales are considered the *profile scales*, with the first three—adjustment, achievement, and intellectual screening—considered the *cognitive triad*.

Skill 3.3   **Demonstrating knowledge of how to select and administer comprehensive, unbiased formal and informal assessments, including assessments of students from culturally and linguistically diverse backgrounds**

IDEA regulations specifically target the over-representation of minority students and students from diverse language and cultural backgrounds among those diagnosed with disabilities and referred for special education services.

FAIR ASSESSMENT PRACTICES

The issue of fair assessment for individuals from minority groups has a long history in law, philosophy, and education. Slavia and Ysseldyke (1995) point out three aspects of this issue that are particularly relevant to the assessment of students.

1. **Representation:** Individuals from diverse backgrounds need to be represented in assessment materials. It is essential that persons from different cultures be represented fairly. Of equal importance is the presentation of individuals from differing genders in nonstereotypical roles and situations.
2. **Acculturation:** It is important that individuals from different backgrounds receive opportunities to acquire the tested skills, information, and values. When students are tested with standardization instruments, they are compared to a set of norms in order to gain an index of their relative standing and to make comparisons (in special education, usually for eligibility or placement decisions). The test assumes that all the students tested have a comparable acculturation; that is, educational, socioeconomic, and experiential background, rather than simply race or ethnicity. (Slavia & Ysseldyke, 1991). Differences in experiential background should therefore be accounted for when administering tests.
3. **Language:** The language and concepts that compose test items should be unbiased. Students should be familiar with the terminology and references used on tests, especially when test results will be used for decision-making purposes.

The wording in federal law is very explicit about the manner in which evaluations must be conducted and about the existence of due process procedures that protect against bias and discrimination. Provisions in the law include the following:

- Testing children in their native or primary language unless it is clearly not feasible to do so. IDEA legislation requires that assessment be not only in a language but also in a form that will give the most accurate picture of a child's abilities or disabilities. Beyond the obvious implications for ESL students, the requirement that it be in the most appropriate form is also significant. Because students with disabilities are often limited in one or another mode of expression or reception of information, a form of response that is fully accessible to the child must also be found.
- The use of evaluation procedures selected and administered to prevent cultural or ethnic discrimination.
- The use of assessment tools validated for the purpose for which they are being used (e.g., achievement levels, IQ scores, adaptive skills).

- Assessment by a multidisciplinary team utilizing several pieces of information to formulate a placement decision. IDEA legislation specifically requires that no single assessment or measurement tool may be used to determine eligibility or placement. This is a critical assessment principle and one that is often overlooked. It is easy to look at the results of one assessment and jump to conclusions about a student's abilities or needs. To get an accurate picture of a child's needs, however, it is necessary to use a variety of measures, and the law requires that educators do so.

All students referred for evaluation for special education should have the results of a relatively current vision and hearing screening on file. This will determine the adequacy of sensory acuity and ensure that learning problems are not due to a vision and/or hearing problem.

Finally, as in all educational endeavors, *confidentiality is a critical requirement.* The Family Educational Rights and Privacy Act of 1974 states that all assessment and discussion of assessment is to be considered strictly confidential and shared only with those immediately involved in decision making and delivery of services to students. Parents have the right to review any and all assessments and their written approval is needed before assessment information can be shared with anyone else (e.g., counselors, outside medical or treatment sources, etc.).

All portions of the special education process, from assessment to placement, are strictly confidential to the people who will be directly servicing the student. Under no circumstances should information be shared outside of the realm of parent/guardian and those providing related services, without the consent of the parent/guardian. Teachers should be vigilant about confidentiality in the workplace as well. Casual conversations, even with other teachers, would violate confidentiality unless the other teachers play a role in providing services to the child.

COMPETENCY 004   **UNDERSTAND STRATEGIES AND PROCEDURES FOR DEVELOPING, IMPLEMENTING, AND MONITORING INDIVIDUALIZED EDUCATION PROGRAMS (IEPS) AND TRANSITION PLANS**

Skill 4.1   **Demonstrating knowledge of how to interpret and communicate the results of formal and informal assessments to students, families, teachers, and other professionals and recommend appropriate services and interventions based on those results**

ABILITY TO INTERPRET TEST RESULTS IN LAYMAN'S TERMS

The special educator must be able to communicate assessment results with language that is understandable to a variety of individuals. These individuals may include parents or guardians, paraprofessionals, professionals in general education, administration, and (in the case of older students) even the student him or herself.

A review of assessment and evaluation results may be done during an IEP meeting in which the formal test lingo is used but paired with an interpretation in layman's terms. Results may also be done in the form of a written report.

ABILITY TO REPRESENT TEST RESULTS AND EDUCATIONAL IMPLICATIONS IN WRITTEN FORMAT

Although the school psychologist often completes student evaluations and writes a report, this may be the task of the special educator when assessment is done in the classroom, in preparation for the student's annual review. In this case, the special education teacher will be asked to write a report summarizing assessment findings and educational implications. The teacher should be able to organize the data in a concise, readable format. Such a report comprises the following:

- Identifying information (student name, age, date of birth, address, gender)
- Reason for assessment
- Test administration information (date, time, duration of test, response of student)
- Test results
- Summary of educational recommendations

Skill 4.2   **Recognizing the continuum of placements and services available for students with disabilities**

Once a student is identified as being *at-risk* academically or socially, remedial interventions are attempted within the regular classroom. Federal legislation requires that sincere efforts be made to help the child learn in the regular classroom.

In some states, school-based teams of educators are formed to solve learning and behavior problems in the regular classroom. These informal problem-solving teams have a variety of names that include concepts of support (school support teams, student support teams), assistance (teacher assistant teams, school assistance teams, or building assistance teams), and appraisal (school appraisal teams). (Pugach & Johnson 1989b).

Regardless of what the teams are called, their purpose is similar. Chalfant, Pysh, and Moultrie (1979) state that *teacher assistance teams* are created to make professional suggestions about curricular alternatives and instructional modifications. These teams may be composed of a variety of participants, including regular education teachers, building administrators, guidance counselors, special education teachers, and the student's parent(s). The team composition varies based on the type of referral, the needs of the student, and availability of educational personnel and state requirements.

Instructional modifications are tried in an attempt to accommodate the student in the regular classroom. Effective instruction is geared toward individual needs and recognizes differences in how students learn. Modifications are tailored to individual student needs. Some strategies for modifying regular classroom instruction shown in the table below are effective with at-risk students with disabilities and students without learning or behavior problems.

Strategies for Modifying Classroom Instruction

Strategy 1 **Provide active learning experiences to teach concepts.** Student motivation is increased when students can manipulate, weigh, measure, read, or write using materials and skills that relate to their daily lives. In addition, retention is better when new learning is related to existing knowledge.

Strategy 2 **Provide ample opportunities for guided practice of new skills.** Frequent feedback on performance is essential to overcome student feelings of inadequacy. Peer tutoring and cooperative projects provide nonthreatening practice opportunities. Individual student conferences, curriculum-based tests, and small group discussions are three useful methods for checking progress.

Strategy 3 **Provide multisensory learning experiences.** Students with learning problems sometimes have sensory processing difficulties; for instance, an auditory discrimination problem may cause misunderstanding about teacher expectations. Lessons and directions that include visual, auditory, tactile, and kinesthetic modes are preferable to a single sensory approach. Such an approach also helps students with learning disabilities that impact abstract learning.

Strategy 4 **Present information in a manner that is relevant to the student.** Particular attention to this strategy is needed when a cultural or economic gap exists between the lives of teachers and students. Relate instruction to a youngster's daily experience and interests.

Strategy 5   **Provide students with concrete illustrations of their progress.** Students with learning problems need frequent reinforcement for their efforts. Charts, graphs, and check sheets provide tangible markers of student achievement.

Evaluation

If instructional modifications in the regular classroom have not proven successful, a student may be referred for multidisciplinary evaluation. The evaluation is comprehensive and includes:

- Norm and criterion-referenced tests (e.g., IQ and diagnostic tests)
- Curriculum-based assessment
- Systematic teacher observation (e.g., behavior frequency checklist)
- Samples of student work
- Parent interviews

The purpose of the evaluation is twofold: to determine eligibility for special education services, and to identify a student's strengths and weaknesses in order to plan an individual education program.

Skill 4.3   **Demonstrating knowledge of how to use assessment information to make appropriate eligibility, program, and placement recommendations for students with disabilities, including those from culturally and linguistically diverse backgrounds**

MAKING INSTRUCTIONAL DECISIONS BASED ON ASSESSMENT RESULTS

Assessment is the key to providing differentiated and appropriate instruction to all students, and this is the area in which teachers will most often use assessment. Teachers should use a variety of assessment techniques to determine the existing knowledge, skills, and needs of each student. Depending on the age of the student and the subject matter under consideration, diagnosis of readiness may be accomplished through pretest, checklists, teacher observation, or student self-report. *Diagnosis serves two related purposes—to identify those students who are not ready for the new instruction and to identify for each student what prerequisite knowledge is lacking.*

Student assessment is an integral part of the teaching-learning process. Identifying student, teacher, or program weaknesses is only significant if the information so obtained is used to remedy those concerns. Lesson materials and lesson delivery must be evaluated to determine relevant prerequisite skills and abilities. *The teacher must be capable of determining whether a student's difficulties lie with the new information, with a lack of significant prior knowledge, or with a core learning disability that must be addressed with specialized lesson plans or accommodations. The ultimate goal of any diagnostic or assessment endeavor is improved learning.* Thus, instruction is adapted to the needs of the learner based on assessment information.

USING ASSESSMENT INFORMATION TO MODIFY PLANS AND ADAPT INSTRUCTION

Assessment skills should be an integral part of teacher training. Teachers are able to use pre- and post-assessments of content areas to monitor student learning, analyze assessment data in terms of individualized support for students and instructional practice for teachers, and design lesson plans that have measurable outcomes and definitive learning standards. *Assessment information should be used to provide performance-based criteria and academic expectations for all students in evaluating whether students have learned the expected skills and content of the subject area.*

Teachers can use assessments to determine whether students have sufficient prior knowledge to engage in a proposed lesson. For example, in an Algebra I class, a teacher might administer a pre-assessment on algebraic expression to ascertain whether the lesson plan should be modified to include a unit on pre-algebraic expression in order to refresh student understanding of that content. The teacher can then create, if needed, quantifiable data to advocate the need of additional resources to support student learning. Once the teacher has taught the unit on algebraic expression, a post-assessment test can be used to test student learning, and a mastery examination can be used to test how well students understand and can apply the knowledge to the next unit of math content learning.

A teacher working with students with learning disabilities will use assessment information in additional ways. For example, if assessments show that a student has extreme difficulty organizing information in the visual field, a teacher may modify a worksheet in math to present only one problem positioned in a large, squared-off field, with lots of white space around it, or perhaps set up problems to be presented individually on 4x6 inch cards, etc.

By analyzing the various types of assessments, teachers can gather more definitive information on projected student academic performance. Instructional strategies for teachers would provide learning targets for student behavior, cognitive thinking skills, and processing skills that can be employed to diversify student learning opportunities.

Standardized tests will have very specific instructions regarding procedures for administration, and it is the teacher's responsibility to see that these standardized procedures are followed. Failure to follow them will invalidate the resulting scores and make it impossible to correctly interpret the results. Some standardized tests also have lists of accommodations that can be used for students with special needs, and these must be carefully recorded, and rules about their use must be strictly followed.

Even with informal assessments, teachers should be attentive to the procedures for administration and should record differences in administration to different students, so that results can be correctly interpreted.

It is important that the results of any formal assessments be correctly interpreted. Most standardized tests will explain how to interpret results so the teacher does not make errors and assume that a test result means something it does not mean.

Particular care must be taken in interpreting some tests. Intelligence test scores, for example, should be interpreted in terms of performance and not the person's potential. The teacher must read the test manuals and become familiar with the following items:

- **Areas measured:** verbal, quantitative, memory, cognitive skills, or the multiple intelligences on some assessments.
- **Population:** target age groups, lack of cultural bias, adaptations or norms for children with physical handicaps such as blindness.
- **Standardization information:** mean and standard deviation, scaled scores and what they mean.
- **Means of comparing performance among subtests**: such as the Verbal and Performance IQ scores of the WISC-IV
- **Uses of the results:** the test manual will contain information about how the results can be used (e.g., using the K-ABC-II to identify gifted children), or how they are not to be used (e.g., assuming that a 3rd grade student who gets a score like a 5th grader on a 3rd grade test is ready to do 5th grade work, an assumption that would not be correct).
- **Information on use with special populations**: such as Spanish-speaking students, students with visual impairments, physical impairments, or learning disabilities.
- **Information concerning reliability and validity**

Skill 4.4 **Demonstrating knowledge of procedures for establishing case records, including how to write assessment team summaries, technically sound IEPs, transition plans, and behavioral plans**

A student with a disability may require specialized instructional methods, use of specific technology, and/or other accommodations. These will be outlined in the student's IEP and should be familiar to all educators and staff members working with the student.

In-services and workshops are often used to explain the above needs of a student to a group of professionals. These sessions may be conducted by the special education teacher. In some instances, the special educator may call upon another professional to conduct the in-service, or he or she may work with the other professional to make a joint presentation. This is sometimes the case with hearing impaired students, when the audiologist conducts an in-service on how the loss impacts classroom performance and how to use auditory training equipment. Another example might be an assistive technology consultant explaining the use of an augmentative communication device.

Explanation of disability and student IEP is important so that everyone working with the student is aware of and focusing on the same goals and objectives. Oftentimes, the general education teacher or other school staff will be listed as implementers of some of the IEP goals and objectives. These individuals should be aware not only of the goals but should also be knowledgeable about how to keep record of student progress. The special educator is responsible for making sure that an appropriate type of documentation is being kept. He or she will often need to provide a chart or questionnaire to assist with this. *Confidentiality is crucial and should be stressed when explaining the student's IEP, as well as addressing where (in a locked file cabinet) it should be kept.*

Observation of the special education teacher is often helpful for those who will be working with the special education student. If the IEP is discussed prior to such an observation, it will help the general education teacher be aware of what to watch for and be prepared to formulate questions for clarification later.

Observation of the general education teacher or other service provider and feedback is helpful once the student is in the general education setting or working with other service providers. The special educator can give feedback on the accommodations and methods being used as well as the student's progress. Observation of the student in these settings provides data needed for future IEP planning, and the feedback of the special educator assists the general education teacher in meeting the needs of the student.

Ongoing evaluation of student progress via the general education teacher can be done in a number of ways in addition to observation. The special education teacher may provide a questionnaire or checklist for the general education teacher. Also, conversations and e-mails on student progress should be documented for reference in completing student progress reports and in IEP planning. *It is the role of the special educator to communicate the importance of input from the general education teacher for these purposes.*

TRANSITION PLANNING

Transition planning is necessary whenever a student transitions or changes from one program or setting to another, throughout life.

TRANSITIONING TO AND THROUGHOUT SCHOOL

Federal, State and local requirements for transition planning services are broken down for the Individualized Family Service Plan (IFSP) and Individualized Education Program (IEP). The IFSP provides early intervention services planning and documentation for an infant or toddler with a disability from birth to three years of age and his or her family. It also prepares all parties for the IEP process, which provides special education services planning and documentation for school-aged students (aged three to twenty-one years) with exceptionalities.

The IFSP and the IEP should address the needs of students as they move from preschool to school, from grade to grade, and (in some cases) from program to program within the school setting. The participants in the transition process include:

- Children and their families
- Service coordinators
- Early intervention practitioners involved in a child's future/pending/current IFSP program
- IFSP teams and preschool teachers
- Early childhood special educators
- Related services practitioners
- Administrators
- Future/pending/current IEP teams

In order to facilitate transition success among these diverse groups of participants, skilled cross-agency communication with achievement-based collaboration is required. Communication and collaboration are frequently quoted as the most significant challenges from people involved in the transition process.

According to the National Early Childhood Transition Center (NECTC), individuals with disabilities experience the same difficulties with transitions as individuals who develop typically, but often to an even higher degree. Goals should be written that will support important aspects in proactive transitioning from one program of development to another for the individuals and their families. In addition to the overall purpose of reducing stress and helping all parties experience success in the new setting, the following are important transition principles:

- Services should be uninterrupted; appropriate services, equipment, and trained staff should be available in new settings
- Transition should avoid any duplication in assessment and goal planning.
- Transition should be marked by ongoing communication and collaborative partnerships.
- Transition should be viewed as a process.
- Transition should meet legal requirements and make decisions in a timely manner.

- Transition should model non-confrontational and effective advocacy that families can emulate throughout their children's lives.

The NECTC scrutinizes and authenticates strategies involved in both early and later childhood transitioning and has made the following suggestions to improve transition at all levels:

- A regular routine/schedule will help promote successful transitioning and will provide the child with a sense of predictability and routine.
- Broad community support results in the highest quality of services for ongoing education and transitioning of children.
- Visiting the new setting in advance and meeting peers and staff improves success.
- Staff from sending and receiving programs must communicate with and, if possible, visit one another and the child's family.
- Transition strategies should be tailored to meet individual needs rather than a generic procedure designed to fit all students.

TRANSITIONING TO POST-SECONDARY LIFE

Transition planning is mandated in the Individuals with Disabilities Education Act (IDEA). This section will cover practical aspects of the process and an overview of transition services. The above comments about transitioning within the school setting are also applicable to transitioning out of school and into the adult world.

Transition planning and services focus on a coordinated set of *student-centered* activities designed to facilitate progression from school to post-school activities. Others involved in post-school transition planning include parents, secondary personnel, post-secondary personnel, counselors, and any relevant community personnel, organizations, company representatives, vocational education instructors, and job coaches; all may be members of the transition team. Transition planning should be flexible and should focus on the developmental and educational requirements of each individual student.

It is important that the student play a key role in transition planning. This entails asking the student to identify preferences and interests and to attend meetings on transition planning. The degree of success experienced by the student in post-secondary educational settings depends on the student's degree of motivation, independence, self-direction, self-advocacy, and academic abilities developed in high school *(see Skill 8.3)*.

In order to contribute to the transition planning process, the student should:

- Understand his or her disability and the impact it has on learning and work; implement achievable goals

- Present a positive self-image by emphasizing strengths while understanding the impact of the disability
- Know how and when to discuss and ask for needed accommodations
- Seek instructors and learning environments that are supportive
- Establish an ongoing personal file that consists of school and medical records, an individualized education program (IEP), a resume, and samples of academic work

The primary role of parents during transition planning is to encourage and assist students in planning and achieving their educational goals. Parents should also encourage students to cultivate independent decision-making and self-advocacy skills.

Also see Skill 1.2.

Skill 4.5   Demonstrating knowledge of systematic procedures for compiling data on a student or group of students for the purpose of continuous program evaluation and improvement

ANECDOTAL RECORDS

These records are notes recorded by the teacher regarding an area of interest or concern involving a particular student. They should focus on observable behaviors and should be descriptive in nature. They should not include assumptions or speculations regarding affective areas such as motivation or interest. These records are usually compiled over a period of several days to several weeks.

PORTFOLIO ASSESSMENT

The use of *student portfolios* for some aspect of assessment has become quite common. The purpose, nature, and policies of portfolio assessment vary greatly from one setting to another. In general, though, a student's portfolio contains samples of work collected over an extended period. The nature of the subject, age of the student, and scope of the portfolio all contribute to the specific mechanics of analyzing, synthesizing, and otherwise evaluating the portfolio contents.

In most cases, the student and teacher make joint decisions concerning which work samples go into the student's portfolio. A collection of work compiled over an extended time allows teacher, student, and parents to view the student's progress from a unique perspective. Qualitative changes over time can be readily apparent from work samples. Such changes are difficult to establish with strictly quantitative records typical of the scores recorded in the teacher's grade book.

QUESTIONING

One of the most frequently occurring forms of assessment in the classroom is oral questioning by the teacher. As the teacher questions the students, she collects a great deal of information about the degree of student learning and potential sources of confusion for the students. While questioning is often viewed as a component of instructional methodology, it is also a powerful assessment tool.

DOMAIN III	PROMOTING STUDENT DEVELOPMENT AND LEARNING
COMPETENCY 005	UNDERSTAND STRATEGIES AND PROCEDURES FOR PLANNING, MANAGING, AND MODIFYING THE LEARNING ENVIRONMENT FOR STUDENTS WITH DISABILITIES, INCLUDING STRATEGIES FOR BEHAVIOR MANAGEMENT

Skill 5.1   Applying knowledge of strategies for teaching students with disabilities in a variety of environments (e.g., one-on-one setting, small group, general education classroom)

Instructional alternatives to help students with learning problems may be referred to as compensatory techniques, instructional adaptations, accommodations, or modifications. A problem-solving approach to determining what modifications should be made centers around the following:

1. The requirements of the course (often state or local standards and objectives)
2. The requirement(s) that the student is not meeting
3. Factors interfering with the student's meeting the requirements
4. Identification of possible modifications or accommodations

Many of the adaptations and modifications helpful to students with disabilities can be seen in terms of Cummins' (1994) analysis of the cognitive demands of a task or lesson. Such adaptations can be designed to either lighten the cognitive burden of a task or make it easier for the student to carry that burden. Cummins' work with students with *limited English proficiency (LEP)* led him to analyze tasks in terms of two variables: *amount of context*, and *cognitive demand.* Lessons or tasks that have a lot of context for a student will be easier for that student than tasks with little or no context. The more context, the easier the task.

Cognitive demand is a measure of how much information must be processed quickly. A cognitively demanding task requires processing lots of information all at once or in rapid succession and is more demanding or difficult. Cognitively undemanding tasks or lessons present only single pieces of information or concepts to process, and they separate tasks or lessons into discrete, small steps. When making changes to accommodate students with special needs, it is helpful to focus on changes that will move the task or lesson from a cognitively demanding, low-context arena to one of high context and reduced cognitive demand.

Adaptations or changes designed to help the student(s) meet the requirements of a class or standard can take place in a number of areas of curriculum and setting. The following are some of the primary areas in which a special education teacher may need to make changes:

- The learning environment
- Methods of instruction and presentation
- Materials and texts
- Lesson content
- Assessment and testing
- Use of assistive technology
- Staff collaboration.

ADAPTING THE OVERALL INSTRUCTIONAL ENVIRONMENT

The teacher can modify the classroom instructional environment in several ways.

Individual Student Variables

Some students with disabilities benefit from sitting close to the teacher or away from windows. Others (with ADHD, for example) might benefit from wiggle seats or fiddle objects, others from an FM system or cubicles that reduce distractions. Seating that reduces distractions serves also to reduce the cognitive load of lessons, by removing the need for the students to block distractions themselves.

Classroom Organization

Many students with learning disabilities benefit from a highly structured environment in which physical areas (e.g., supplies, reading, math, and writing) are clearly labeled and a schedule for the day is prominently displayed. Individual schedule charts can be useful if some students follow different schedules, such as leaving for a resource room or specialized therapy periodically. Such schedules reduce the cognitive load required to simply get through the day, and provide increased context for the student navigating the daily routine.

The teacher can also vary grouping arrangements (e.g., large group, small group, peer tutoring, or learning centers) with student needs in mind. Five basic types of grouping arrangements are typically used in the classroom:

Large Group with Teacher

Examples of appropriate activities include show and tell, discussions, watching plays or movies, brainstorming ideas, and playing games. In general education classrooms science, social studies, and most content area subjects are taught in large groups. The advantage of large-group instruction is that it is time-efficient and prepares students for higher levels of secondary and post-secondary education settings. However, with large groups, instruction cannot be as easily differentiated or tailored to individual student needs or learning styles. Mercer and Mercer (1985) recommend the following guidelines for effective large-group instruction:

- Keep instruction short, ranging from 5 to 15 minutes for first grade to seventh grade; 5 to 40 minutes for grades 8 to 12.
- Use questions to involve all students, use lecture-pause routines, and encourage active participation among the lower-performing students.
- Incorporate visual aids to promote understanding and maintain a lively pace.
- Break up the presentation with different rates of speaking, giving students a "stretch break," varying voice volume, etc.
- Establish rules of conduct for large groups and praise students who follow the rules.

When students with special needs are included in large group instruction, care must be taken to conduct the activity with their needs in mind. For example, if a particular student has a limited recall or understanding of a subject, it can be useful to ask the student a concrete question or let the student answer before anyone else so his/her answer is not "taken" by someone else. Choral responses regarding key points can help provide context and support for students with some disabilities, as well.

Small Group Instruction

Small group instruction usually includes five to seven students and is recommended for teaching basic academic skills such as math facts or reading, and for introducing many abstract content area concepts. This model is especially effective for students with learning problems. Composition of the groups should be flexible to accommodate different rates of progress through instruction. Some of the advantages of teaching in small groups are that the teacher is better able to tailor the instruction to the special needs of certain students, to provide feedback, monitor student progress, and give more individual attention and praise. With small groups, the teacher must provide a steady pace for the lesson, provide questions and activities that allow all to participate, and include lots of positive praise. Small groups can also make differentiated instruction easier and more practical.

One Student with Teacher

One-to-one tutorial teaching can be used to provide extra assistance to individual students. Such tutoring may be scheduled at set times during the day or provided as the need arises. The tutoring model is typically found more often in elementary and resource classrooms than in secondary settings, and is particularly effective for students with certain disabilities.

Peer Tutoring

In an effective peer tutoring arrangement, the teacher trains the peer tutors and matches them with students who need extra practice and assistance. In addition to academic skills, the arrangement can help both students work on social skills such as cooperation and self-esteem. Both students may be working on the same material or the tutee may be working to strengthen areas of weakness. The teacher determines the target goals, selects the material, sets up the guidelines, trains the student tutors in the rules and methods of the sessions, and monitors and evaluates the sessions. Care must be taken, however, to avoid the appearance that some students are smarter than others and that the "smarter" students have more work because of the "slower" students. It can be very helpful if the teacher can find something that allows the tutee in one situation to act as tutor in another.

Cooperative Learning

Cooperative learning differs from peer tutoring in that students are grouped in teams or small groups and the methods are based on teamwork, individual accountability, and team reward. Individual students are responsible for their own learning and share of the work, as well as the group's success. As with peer tutoring, the goals, target skills, materials, and guidelines are developed by the teacher. Teamwork skills may also be taught. By focusing on team goals, all members of the team are encouraged to help each other as well as to improve their individual performance. When students with disabilities are included in such cooperative teams it is imperative that the teacher arrange the tasks so that there is something substantive and important for each member of the group to contribute.

Skill 5.2   Demonstrating knowledge of strategies for planning and managing the learning environment for students with disabilities (e.g., fostering students' independence, designing consistent daily routines, establishing behavioral expectations, maintaining students' attention)

CLASSROOM MANAGEMENT

The teacher can vary grading systems, reinforcement systems, and even the rules to accommodate the varying needs of the students. Early teaching and practice of daily classroom routines can be particularly helpful to students with certain learning disabilities or emotional problems. It may be helpful to pay extra attention to the transitions between tasks, lessons, or parts of the day. Some students benefit from having clear stimuli (e.g., a bell, hand signal, or flag,) to signal changes and transitions. Attention and time spent on such routines early in the year can pay big dividends in classroom management later in the year. The specific techniques required will depend upon the needs of the students.

METHODS OF PRESENTATION OF SUBJECT MATTER

The teacher can vary the method of presentation of new material in many ways depending upon the specific needs of the students. In general, subject matter should be presented in a fashion that helps students *organize, understand,* and *remember* important information. Students with learning disabilities will often benefit from hands-on, multimodal presentation and interaction with new concepts and materials. It is helpful if the goal of the lesson, and the most important points are clearly stated at the start. Students with learning disabilities also benefit from material that is presented one concept at a time (this reduces cognitive demand). Advance organizers and other instructional devices can:

- Connect information to what is already known (increases context)
- Make abstract ideas more concrete (reduces cognitive demand)
- Capture students' interest in the material
- Help students organize the information and visualize the relationships (increases context and reduces demand)

Organizers can be such visual aids as diagrams, tables, charts, guides, or verbal cues that alert students to the nature and content of the lesson. Organizers may be used:

- **Before the lesson** to alert the student to the main point of the lesson, establish a rationale for learning, and activate background information
- **During the lesson** to help students organize information, keep focused on important points, and aid comprehension
- **At the close of the lesson** to summarize and remember important points

Examples of organizers include the following:

- Question and graphic-oriented study guide
- Concept diagramming: students brainstorm a concept and organize information into three lists (always present, sometimes present, and never present).
- Semantic feature analysis: students construct a table with examples of the concept in one column and important features or characteristics in the opposite column. This table can involve words, pictures, or even concrete objects, as necessary to meet the individual student's needs.
- Semantic webbing: The concept (in word, picture or object) is placed in the middle of the chart or chalkboard and relevant information is placed around it. Lines show the relationships. Color coding and letting students physically attach string or pipe cleaners to make the web can increase context and make the conceptual relationships more concrete.
- Memory (mnemonic) devices
- Diagrams, charts, and tables

INSTRUCTIONAL MATERIALS

In many school systems, the textbooks and primary instructional materials have been chosen by the school, though the teacher may also be able to select additional materials. Although specialized materials for certain special needs (e.g., large print or CDs for students with visual disabilities or dyslexia) may be available, it is usually necessary for the teachers to modify instructional materials and texts for their students with special needs. It may be necessary to enlarge the print on a worksheet or text not available in large print, or to provide additional diagrams or rearrange text on the page for students with organizational difficulties. Students with certain visual or writing difficulties may not be able to copy math problems from a book, or may need larger numbers or space for their work.

Though the specific modifications will depend upon individual student needs, one of the most common requirements will be finding or revising text for learners who cannot read at grade level or who have difficulty comprehending what they read in content areas such as science and social studies. The most common specific learning disabilities involve reading difficulties. In order for such students to have equal access to the grade-level curriculum in content areas, it is often necessary to revise printed materials so students can access them at their reading comprehension level. Whether selecting published materials, or revising them for the students, these guidelines should be followed in order to increase context, reduce cognitive demand, and provide content material that students with learning disabilities can access:

- Avoid complex sentences with many relative clauses.
- Avoid the passive tense.
- Try to make the topic sentence the first sentence in a paragraph.
- Make sure paragraphs have a concluding sentence that restates the topic sentence in another way.
- Use simple, declarative sentences that have only one main idea or concept at a time.
- Use simple, single syllable, concrete words rather than more complex words (e.g., "an arduous journey" should be "a hard trip").
- Eliminate nonessential information in favor of the main concepts necessary to teach.
- Try to use only one tense in all the sentences.
- Add diagrams and illustrations whenever possible, and deliver information through labels rather than complete sentences.
- Whenever possible, include multisensory elements and multimodalities in the presentation.
- Avoid unfamiliar names and terms that will "tie up" the students' cognitive efforts (e.g., while the student is trying to figure out how to read the name " Aloysius" he or she will miss the point of the sentence; change the name to "Al")

METHODS OF PRACTICE AND RETENTION

Many of the common review and practice methods used in general education classrooms are suitable for students with special needs. Others will need modification. Each daily lesson should begin with a review of the important facts, rules, and concepts of the previous lesson. *The review may incorporate questions from the teacher, a brief quiz, checking homework, and feedback on homework.* On the basis of the students' responses to the questions, the teacher can adjust the instruction of the lesson to go over areas that were not mastered or retained.

Reviews of the lesson can also be in the in the form of a synopsis and teacher questioning at the end of the lesson to see whether the students have learned the material. At the beginning of the next day, if the teacher sees that the students responded correctly at the end of the previous lesson, but not in the day-after review, they may need to work on retention strategies. Students with certain learning disabilities may need to "over learn" new material. Additional practice and review may be necessary for them. The teacher may need to alter the amount or content of material to be practiced (limit it to the most essential concepts or skills, for example), the time allowed for practice, or the methods used. Some students may have disabilities that impact their ability to recall information, for example, and their practice may need to involve recognition rather than recall. *Many students with learning disabilities need heavy teacher scaffolding support when a skill or concept is first introduced.* They may also need a more gradual reduction of scaffolding than their peers without disabilities, in order to retain the information.

Homework provides review opportunities for independent practice. Review should be done on a daily basis, with weekly and monthly cumulative reviews to provide information on retention of knowledge and opportunities to "over learn" the materials. It may be necessary to modify the homework assigned to students with learning disabilities. In many cases students with certain learning or emotional disabilities cannot handle the same level of homework as students without disabilities. In addition, parents may or may not have the skills necessary to help practice the highly specialized lessons some children with learning disabilities need (e.g., specialized phoneme awareness practice).

Students can also review and practice skills in peer tutoring, cooperative learning arrangements, and individual student seatwork. When errors are observed, teachers should find opportunities to teach the materials again. By immediately correcting the errors, the student is not inadvertently reinforced for the wrong process. Opportunities to reteach can also appear in student questions about present material that refer back to previous material.

LESSON CONTENT

Although the content of the curriculum is usually dictated by state or local standards, the teacher of students with special needs will often need to modify the content through differentiated instruction in order for the students to access it. Modifications in curriculum are sometimes required by a student's IEP. In addition, student learning disabilities may require the teacher to modify the lesson content in order to reduce the cognitive demands on the student.

ASSESSMENT

Teachers of students with special needs will frequently find it necessary to modify their assessment techniques and procedures in order to accurately assess the students' knowledge and skills. This section lists common kinds of accommodations and modifications needed in special education.

Because certain disabilities can interfere with performance on an assessment, it is often necessary for the teacher to break down the task or skill and test each part separately. Many of the common accommodations and modifications in testing are designed to separate the specific skill or knowledge being tested from some other ability or skill impacted by a disability. For example, when testing a student with dyslexia on retention of a concept in science, it would be inappropriate to use a reading/writing assessment. The student's response to a written test would be confounded by the inability to read the test or to compose readable written responses. In such cases an oral exam might more accurately assess the student's science knowledge.

Accommodations or modifications in assessment usually fall into the following categories:

- **Setting:** Changes in the location of the testing, such as separate seating or room, special lighting or noise buffers, adaptive furniture, small group or one-to-one testing
- **Timing and Scheduling:** Changes in the duration or time of the test such as allowing extra time or an absence of time limits, frequent breaks, or scheduling the test at a time of day when a student functions best—has had specific medication, etc.
- **Presentation of Test:** Changes in how the test is given to a student, such as oral testing, large print or Braille, sign language, colored overlays or special paper, etc. This would also include allowing the teacher to clarify directions or read the test to the student.
- **Student Responses:** Changes in how the student is allowed to respond to the test, such as allowing oral responses, multiple choice rather than essay, dictating open responses, use of assistive devices such as computer keyboards, spell checkers, writing software, etc.

In many cases such accommodations and modifications will be specified in a student's IEP, and the teacher is legally responsible to see that the required accommodations are made both in classroom assessments and in district wide testing.

Skill 5.3   **Applying knowledge of strategies for developing, implementing, modifying, and monitoring classroom behavior management plans for students with disabilities, including strategies for providing individual and school-wide positive behavioral supports**

Classroom management plans should be in place when the school year begins. Developing a management plan takes a proactive approach—that is, deciding on what behaviors will be expected of the class as a whole, anticipating possible problems, and teaching the behaviors early in the school year.

Behavior management techniques should focus on positive procedures that can be used at home as well as at school. Involving the students in the development of the classroom rules lets the students know the rationale for the rules and allows them to assume responsibility for them. Once the rules are established, enforcement and reinforcement for following the rules should begin right away.

Consequences should be introduced at the same time as the rules. They should be clearly stated and understood by all of the students. The severity of the consequence should match the severity of the offense and must be enforceable. The teacher must apply the consequence consistently and fairly; students should know what to expect when they choose to break a rule.

Like consequences, students should understand what rewards to expect for following the rules. The teacher should never promise a reward that cannot be delivered. The teacher should also follow through with the reward as soon as possible. Consistency and fairness are necessary for rewards to be effective. Students will become frustrated and give up if they see that rewards and consequences are not delivered timely and fairly.

About four to six classroom rules should be posted where students can easily see and read them. These rules should be stated positively and describe specific behaviors so they are easy to understand. Certain rules may also be tailored to meet target goals and IEP requirements of individual students. (For example, a new student who has had problems with leaving the classroom may need an individual behavior contract to assist him or her with adjusting to the class rule about remaining in the assigned area.) As the students demonstrate the behaviors, the teacher should provide reinforcement and corrective feedback. Periodic "refresher" practice can be done as needed, for example, after a long holiday or if students begin to "slack off." A copy of the classroom plan should be readily available for substitute use, and the classroom aide should also be familiar with the plan and procedures.

The teacher should clarify and model the expected behavior for the students. In addition to the classroom management plan, a management plan should be developed for special situations, (e.g., fire drills) and transitions (e.g., going to and from the cafeteria). A periodic review of the rules, as well as modeling and practice, may be conducted as needed (such as after an extended school holiday).

Procedures that use social humiliation, withholding of basic needs, pain, or extreme discomfort should never be used in a behavior management plan.

Emergency intervention procedures used when the student is a danger to him or herself or others are not considered behavior management procedures. Throughout the year, the teacher should periodically review the types of interventions being used, assess the effectiveness of the interventions used in the management plan, and make revisions as needed for the best interests of each child.

MOTIVATION

Before the teacher begins instruction, he or she should choose activities that are meaningful, relevant, and at the appropriate level of student difficulty. Teacher behaviors that motivate students include the following:

- Maintaining success expectations through teaching, goal setting, establishing connections between effort and outcome, and self-appraisal and reinforcement.
- Having a supply of intrinsic incentives, such as rewards, appropriate competition between students, and the value of the academic activities.
- Focusing on students' intrinsic motivation through adapting the tasks to students' interests, providing opportunities for active response, including a variety of tasks, providing rapid feedback, incorporating games into the lesson, and allowing students the opportunity to make choices, create, and interact with peers.
- Stimulating students' learning by modeling positive expectations and attributions. Project enthusiasm and personalize abstract concepts. Students will be better motivated if they know what they will be learning. The teacher should also model problem solving and task-related thinking so students can see how the process is done.

For adolescents, motivation strategies are usually aimed at getting the student actively involved in the learning process. Since the adolescent has the opportunity to get involved in a wider range of activities outside the classroom (e.g., job, car, being with friends), stimulating motivation may be the focus even more than academics.

Motivation may be achieved through extrinsic reinforcers or intrinsic reinforcers. This is accomplished by allowing the student a degree of choice in what is being taught or how it will be taught. The teacher should, if possible, obtain a commitment either through a verbal or written contract between the student and the teacher. Adolescents also respond to regular feedback, especially when that feedback shows that they are making progress.

Rewards for adolescents often include free time for listening to music, recreation, or games. They may like extra time for a break or exemption from a homework assignment. They may receive rewards at home for satisfactory performance at school. Other rewards include self-charting progress and tangible reinforcers. In summary, motivational activities may be used for goal setting, self-recording of academic progress, self-evaluation, and self-reinforcement.

CLASSROOM INTERVENTIONS

Classroom interventions anticipate student disruptions and nullify potential discipline problems. Every student is different and each situation is unique; therefore, student behavior cannot be matched to specific interventions. Good classroom management requires the ability to select appropriate interventions strategies from an array of alternatives. The following nonverbal and verbal interventions were explained in Henley, Ramsey, and Algonzzine (1993):

- **Nonverbal intervention:** The use of nonverbal interventions allows classroom activities to proceed without interruption. These interventions also enable teachers to avoid "power struggles" with students.
- **Body language:** Teachers can convey authority and command respect through body language. Posture, eye contact, facial expressions, and gestures are examples of body components that signal leadership to students.
- **Planned ignoring:** Many minor classroom disturbances are best handled through planned ignoring. When teachers ignore attention-seeking behaviors, students often do likewise.
- **Signal interference:** There are numerous nonverbal signals that teachers can use to quiet a class. Some of these are eye contact, snapping fingers, a frown, shaking the head, or making a quieting gesture with the hand. A few teachers present signs like flicking the lights, putting a finger over the lips, or winking at a selective student.
- **Proximity control:** Teachers who move around the room merely need to stand near a student or small group of students, or gently place a hand on a student's shoulder to stop a disturbing behavior. Teachers who stand or sit as if rooted are compelled to issue verbal directions in order to deal with student disruptions.
- **Removal of seductive objects:** Some students become distracted by objects. Removal of those objects may eliminate the need some students have to handle, grab, or touch objects that take the focus of their attention away from instruction.
- **Verbal interventions:** Because nonverbal interventions are the least intrusive, they are generally preferred. Verbal interventions are useful after it is clear that nonverbal interventions have been unsuccessful in preventing or stopping disruptive behavior.
- **Humor:** Some teachers have been successful in dispelling discipline problems with a quip or an easy comment that produces smiles or gentle

laughter from students. *This does not include sarcasm, cynicism, or teasing, which increase tension and often create resentment.*

- **Sane messages:** Sane messages are descriptive and model appropriate behavior. They help students understand how their behavior affects others. "Karol, when you talk during silent reading, you disturb everyone in your group," is an example of a sane message. Communicating such messages privately to students has proven to have a greater effect than when they are given in front of a class.
- **Restructuring:** When confronted with student disinterest, the teacher may make the decision to change activities. This is an example of an occasion when restructuring could be used by the teacher to regenerate student interest.
- **Hypodermic affection:** Sometimes, students get frustrated, discouraged, and anxious in school. Hypodermic affection lets students know they are valued. Saying a kind word, giving a smile, or just showing interest in a child often gives the encouragement that is needed. This is most effective if you do it daily as your students enter your classroom.
- **Praise and encouragement:** Effective praise should be directed at student behavior rather than at the student personally. "Catching a child being good" is an example of an effective use of praise that reinforces positive classroom behavior. Comments like, "You are really trying hard," encourage student effort.
- **Alerting:** Making abrupt changes from one activity to another can bring on behavior problems. Alerting helps students to make smooth transitions by giving them time to make emotional adjustments to change.
- **Accepting student feelings:** Providing opportunities for students to express their feelings—even those that are distressful—helps them to learn to do so in appropriate ways. Role playing, class meetings or discussions, life-space interviews, journal writings, and other creative modes help students to channel difficult feelings into constructive outlets.

SCHEDULE DEVELOPMENT

Schedule development depends on the type of class (elementary or secondary) and the setting (regular classroom or resource room). There are, however, general rules of thumb that apply to both types and settings:

1. Allow time for transitions, planning, and setups.
2. Aim for maximum instructional time by pacing the instruction quickly and allotting time for practice of the new skills.
3. Proceed from short assignments to long ones, breaking up long lessons or complex tasks into short sessions or step-by-step instruction.
4. Follow a less preferred academic or activity with a highly preferred academic activity.
5. In settings where students are working on individualized plans, do not schedule all the students at once in activities that require a great deal of

teacher assistance. For example, have some students work on math or spelling while the teacher works with the students in reading (as it usually requires more teacher involvement).

6. Break up a longer segment into several smaller segments with a variety of activities.

Special Considerations for Elementary Classrooms

1. Determine the amount of time that is needed for activities such as P.E., lunch, or recess.
2. Allow about 15 to 20 minutes each for opening and closing exercises. Spend this time for "housekeeping" activities, such as collecting lunch money, going over the schedule, cleaning up, reviewing the day's activities, and getting ready to go home.
3. Schedule academics for periods when the students are more alert and motivated—usually in the afternoon.
4. Build in time for slower students to finish their work; others may work at learning centers or other activities of interest. Allowing extra time gives the teacher time to give more attention where it is needed, conduct assessments, or allow students to complete or correct work.

Special Considerations for Secondary Classes

Secondary school days are usually divided into five, six, or seven periods of about 50 minutes each, with time for homeroom and lunch. Students cannot stay behind and finish their work since they have to leave for a different room. Resource room time should be scheduled so that the student does not miss academic instruction in his or her classroom or miss desirable nonacademic activities. In schools where ESE teachers also co-teach or work with students in the regular classroom, the regular teacher will have to coordinate lesson plans with those of the special education teacher. Consultation time will also have to be budgeted into the schedule.

Transfer between Classes and Subjects

Effective teachers use class time efficiently. This results in higher student subject engagement and will likely result in more subject matter retention. One way teachers use class time efficiently is through a smooth transition from one activity to another; this activity is also known as "management transition." Management transition is defined as when the "teacher shifts from one activity to another in a systemic, academically oriented way." One factor that contributes to efficient management transition is the teacher's management of instructional material. Effective teachers gather their materials during the planning stage of instruction. In doing this, a teacher avoids flipping through things looking for the items necessary for the current lesson. Momentum is lost and student concentration is broken when this occurs.

Additionally, teachers who keep students informed of the sequencing of instructional activities maintain systematic transitions because the students are prepared to move on to the next activity. For example, the teacher says, "When we finish with this guided practice together, we will turn to page twenty-three and each student will do the exercises. I will then circulate throughout the classroom helping on an individual basis. Okay, let's begin." Following an example such as this will lead to systematic smooth transitions between activities, because the students will be turning to page twenty-three when the class finishes the practice without a break in concentration.

Another method that leads to smooth transitions is to move students in groups and clusters rather than to seat them one-by-one. This is called *group fragmentation*. For example, if some students do seat work while other students gather for a reading group, the teacher moves the students in predetermined groups. Instead of calling the individual names of the reading group, which would be time consuming and laborious, the teacher simply says, "Will the blue reading group please assemble at the reading station. The red and yellow groups will quietly do the vocabulary assignment I am now passing out." As a result of this activity, the classroom is ready to move on in a matter of seconds rather than minutes.

Additionally, the teacher may employ academic transition signals, which are defined as any "teacher utterance that indicate[s] movement of the lesson from one topic or activity to another by indicating where the lesson is and where it is going." For example, the teacher may say, "That completes our description of clouds, now we will examine weather fronts." Like the sequencing of instructional materials, this keeps the student informed on what is coming next so he or she will move to the next activity with little or no break in concentration.

Therefore, *effective teachers manage transitions from one activity to another in a systematically oriented way by efficiently managing instructional matter, sequencing instructional activities, moving students in groups, and employing academic transition signals.* Through an efficient use of class time, achievement is increased because students spend more class time engaged in on-task behavior.

Transition refers to changes in class activities that involve movement. Examples include the following:

1. Breaking up from large group instruction into small groups for learning centers and small-group instructions
2. Moving from the classroom to lunch, to the playground, or to elective classes
3. Finishing reading at the end of one period and getting ready for math the next period
4. Emergency situations such as fire drills

Successful transitions are achieved by using proactive strategies. Early in the year, the teacher pinpoints the transition periods in the day and anticipates possible behavior problems (such as students habitually returning late from lunch). After identifying possible problems with the environment or the schedule, the teacher plans proactive strategies to minimize or eliminate those problems. Proactive planning also gives the teacher the advantage of being prepared, addressing behaviors before they become problems, and incorporating strategies into the classroom management plan right away. Transition plans can be developed for each type of transition and the expected behaviors for each situation taught directly to the students.

Skill 5.4   Demonstrating knowledge of strategies for crisis intervention and prevention

According to the Center for Effective Collaboration and Practice (USDE 1998), most schools are safe; however, violence from surrounding communities has begun to make its way into schools. Fortunately, there are ways to intervene and prevent crisis in our schools.

EARLY WARNING SIGNS

First, administrators, teachers, families, students, support staff, and community leaders must be trained and/or informed about early warning signs that a student might be approaching a crisis breakdown. It should also be emphasized not to use these warning signs to inappropriately label or stigmatize individual students, because they might display some of the following early warning signs:

- Social withdrawal
- Excessive feelings of isolation
- Excessive feelings of rejection
- Being a victim of violence
- Feelings of being picked on and persecuted
- Low school interest and poor academic performance
- Expression of violence in writings and drawings
- Uncontrolled anger
- Patterns of impulsive and chronic hitting, intimidating, and bullying
- History of discipline problems
- Past history of violent and aggressive behavior
- Intolerance for differences and prejudicial attitudes
- Drug use and alcohol use
- Affiliation with gangs
- Inappropriate access to, possession of, and use of firearms
- Serious threats of violence

These early signs mean that teachers should begin to intervene and try to assist the student to identify the problem and find a positive solution.

IMMINENT WARNING SIGNS

Early warning signs and imminent warning signs differ in that imminent warning signs require an immediate response. Imminent warning signs indicate that a student is very close to behaving in a way that is potentially dangerous to self and/or others. Imminent warning signs can include:

- Serious physical fighting with peers or family members
- Severe destruction of property
- Severe rage for seemingly minor reasons
- Detailed threats of lethal violence
- Possession and/or use of firearms and other weapons
- Other self-injurious behaviors or threats of suicide

When imminent signs are seen, school staff must follow the school board policies that are in place. These typically include reporting the warning signs to a designated person or persons. It is the teacher's responsibility to be familiar with the school crisis intervention plans.

INTERVENTION AND PREVENTION PLANS

Every school system's plan might be different, but the plan should be derived from some of the following suggestions.

Share responsibility by establishing a partnership with the child, school, home, and community. Schools should collaborate with community agencies to coordinate the plan. They should also render services to students who might need assistance. The community involvement should include child and family service agencies, law enforcement and juvenile justice systems, mental health agencies, businesses, faith and ethnic leaders, and other community agencies. An important aspect of this at the school level is the establishment of a culture of trust and support among students and staff. If students feel they can trust teachers and staff and feel comfortable discussing sensitive issues with them, they are more likely to provide information about themselves or others that will help staff recognize the early warning signs.

Inform parents and listen to them when early warning signs are observed. Effective and safe schools make persistent efforts to involve parents by informing them routinely about school discipline policies, procedures, and rules; informing them about their children's behavior (both good and bad); involving them in making decisions concerning school-wide disciplinary policies and procedures; and encouraging them to participate in prevention.

Maintain confidentiality and parents' rights to privacy. Parental involvement and consent is required before personally identifiable information is shared with other agencies except in the case of emergencies or suspicion of abuse.

Develop the capacity of staff, students, and families to intervene. Schools should provide the entire school community—teachers, students, parents, and support staff—with training and support in responding to imminent warning signs, preventing violence, and intervening safely and effectively. Interventions must be monitored by professionals who are trained in this area.

Support students in being responsible for their actions. Schools and members of the community should encourage students to see themselves as responsible for their actions and actively engage them in planning, implementing, and evaluating violence prevention initiatives.

Simplify staff requests for urgent assistance. Many school systems and community agencies have complex legalistic referral systems with timelines and waiting lists. This should be a simple process that does not prevent someone from requesting assistance.

Drill and Practice. Most schools are required to have drills and to provide practice to ensure that everyone is informed of proper procedures to follow if emergencies occur. In addition to violence caused by a student, the emergency can also be an intruder in the building, a bomb threat, a natural disaster, or a fire.

COMPETENCY 006   **UNDERSTAND EFFECTIVE CURRICULAR PLANNING AND INSTRUCTIONAL PRACTICES FOR STUDENTS WITH DISABILITIES**

Skill 6.1   **Applying knowledge of how to adapt and modify the general and special education curricula to meet the individual needs of students with disabilities (e.g., providing access to the general curriculum; incorporating functional living, communication, and/or social skills)**

In order for students to apply critical thinking and problem solving skills learned in school to decisions relevant to functional life needs, students must be able to *generalize* or *transfer* these skills from the school setting to the functional living setting of home life, jobs, and leisure. Generalization training is a procedure in which a behavior is reinforced in each of a series of situations until the student begins to more automatically apply the learned behavior to new situations. The more similar two situations are, the easier it is for the student to transfer learned behavior to the new situation.

This is particularly true of functional skills involved in independent living and the workplace. Skills learned in the school setting are far more likely to generalize to home life or the workplace if the school setting resembles the home or work setting.

- Even when the settings are deliberately made as similar as possible, however, many students with disabilities will need instruction specifically designed to help them think about how to apply what they have learned in school to real life problems. These are higher-order or critical thinking skills because they require students to think about thinking. For example, these skills can be found in: Balancing a checkbook and analyzing bills for overcharges
- Comparing shopping ads or catalogue deals
- Following news stories
- Reading a TV guide and planning to record shows
- Gathering information/data from diverse sources to plan a project
- Following a sequence of directions in a recipe or on the job
- Looking for cause and effect relationships (e.g., why is the dog barking or why is the baby crying?)
- Appropriate responses and use of community resources (e.g., call the electrical company if the power is out, call the doctor and my work supervisor if I am sick)
- Evaluating information relevant to making a given decision (e.g., deciding which movie to go to might involve cost, time, duration, personal interest, available transportation)

General techniques for improving the transfer of problem solving skills might be modified as follows:

- Use of the cooperative learning groups or whole-discussions of how to solve problems might involve common home life and job related problems rather than folktales or math. Role playing can be particularly effective in cooperative groups for this purpose.
- Allowing students or groups of students to try their own solutions and then discussing various approaches that might work can help them learn that there may be more than one solution to or method for solving a problem. For example, if the proposed problem is how to get to work on time, solutions might include walking (depending on the distance), biking, a bus route, subway, driving or carpooling, or even a taxi.
- Collaboration among teachers
- Helping students identify similarities in functional problems might involve helping them see that getting to work on time and getting to a movie on time involve many of the same skills, for example.
- A modification of the analysis of math word problems can be used as a general problem-solving strategy for functional life problems. For example, students can ask themselves: what is the problem or decision, or what do I want to do? (main idea)
- What do I need in order to do it? (information needed to solve)
- What do I need to find out that I don't already know? (relevant information)
- How can I find out what I need to know? (strategy or plan)
- Solve the problem or make a decision
- Check to see if decision or solution actually gets me what I wanted

Attention to learner needs during planning is essential. It includes identifying the things students already know or need to know; matching learner needs with instructional elements such as content, materials, activities, and goals; and determining whether or not students have performed at an acceptable level following instruction.

The ability to create a personal chart of students' functional learning and emotional growth found within the performance-based assessment of individualized portfolios can be useful for both students and teachers. Teachers can use semester portfolios to gauge student progress and the personal growth of students who are constantly trying to apply their learning to new situations. When a student studies to master a functional skill and makes a visual of his or her learning, it can help connect the learning to a higher level of thinking that can be generalized to new situations that were not specifically studied in class.

ARRANGING OBJECTIVES TO ENHANCE TRANSFER OF LEARNING

Transfer of learning occurs when experience with one task influences performance on another task. Positive transfer occurs when the required responses and the stimuli are similar, such as moving from baseball to handball or from field hockey to soccer. Negative transfer occurs when the stimuli remain similar but the required responses change, such as shifting from soccer to football, tennis to racquetball, or boxing to sports karate. As mentioned in previous skills, instructional procedures should stress the similar features between the activities and the dimensions that are transferable. Specific information should emphasize when stimuli in the old and new situations are the same and when responses used in the old situation apply to the new.

To facilitate learning, instructional objectives should be arranged according to their patterns of similarity. Objectives involving similar responses should be closely sequenced so the possibility for positive transfer is stressed. Likewise, learning objectives that involve different responses should be programmed to emphasize and explicitly teach the difference to minimize negative transfer.

For example, students should have little difficulty transferring handwriting instruction to writing information on an employment form; however, there might be some negative transfer when moving from manuscript to cursive writing. By using transitional methods and focusing on the similarities between manuscript and cursive writing, negative transfer can be reduced.

When addressing basic skills in the classroom, it is important to keep the ultimate uses of those skills in mind in order to improve positive transfer and minimize negative transfer. For example, the arrangement of many traditional practice worksheets for addition and subtraction could actually produce some negative transfer when applied to a critical life skill: balancing a checkbook. Although column addition is often taught in school, most subtraction problems involve only two numbers at a time. Checkbooks require successive, sequential subtraction; in each case the number obtained as a difference becomes the "starting" number from which the next number is subtracted. Also, the operation switches from subtraction to addition when a deposit is made. Both these processes might be difficult for some students with disabilities. In order to minimize negative transfer, classroom worksheets might need to be modified to include such skills.

COLLABORATION TO ENHANCE GENERALIZATION OF SKILLS

When the goal is to promote students' acquisition of functional life skills, collaboration among various teachers and specialists to provide reinforcement of these generalization skills might involve several teachers working on related skills in different subjects. The strategy of designing math worksheets to reflect functional skills, mentioned above, is one example of collaboration. Others might include the following:

- One functional life skill is getting to work on time. In this instance, the reading teacher might have a lesson on how to read diagrams such as bus and subway lines, while the social studies teacher covers street maps, and the math teacher works on elapsed time using bus and job schedules.

- In a decision-making problem about choosing among possible residences in which to live with your pet dog, the reading teacher might cover reading ads and lease arrangements, the science teacher might include a unit on the physical needs of the pet, social studies might address how to find out about local ordinances, and math could involve costs to support the pet, or even the amount of fencing material (and its cost) for building a fence for the dog.

Skill 6.2   **Applying knowledge of how to monitor, adapt, and modify instruction to meet the individual needs of students with disabilities (e.g., using remedial methods to provide additional instruction and practice, providing accommodations such as assistive technologies, conducting and using task analysis to sequence instruction, using methods to foster students' independence)**

IDEA provides the following definition of an **Assistive Technology** device:
"Any item, piece of equipment or product system, whether acquired commercially off the shelf, modified, or customized that is used to increase, maintain or improve functional capabilities of children with disabilities."

IDEA 2004 clarified that assistive technology "does not include a medical device that is surgically implanted, or the replacement of such device."

Almost anything can be considered assistive technology if it can be used to increase, maintain, or improve the functioning of a person with a disability. Some areas in which Assistive Technology (AT) may be used:

- Communication
- Hearing
- Vision
- Environmental management
- Body movement
- Academic concepts related to reading, writing, or using numbers
- Leisure activities
- Memory
- Work or vocational skills

AT devices can increase the following for a person with a disability:

- Level of independence
- Quality of life
- Productivity
- Performance

- Educational/vocational options
- Success in regular education settings

A variety of AT devices are available to address the functional capabilities of students with disabilities. Zabala (2000) identified AT devices in fourteen major areas.

ACADEMIC AND LEARNING AIDS

Electronic and non-electronic aids such as calculators, spell checkers, portable word processors, and computer-based software solutions that assist the student in academic areas.

Reading

AT solutions that address difficulty with reading may include:

- **Colored overlays:** Overlays that alter the contrast between the text and background are helpful for students with perceptual difficulties. It may be necessary to experiment to determine the best color or combination of colors for a student.
- **Reading window:** A simple, no-tech solution for students who have difficulty with tracking. A "frame" is constructed from tag board or cardboard, allowing the student to see one line of text at a time as he/she moves down the page.
- **Spell checker or talking dictionary:** Students type in words they are having difficulty reading and the device will say the word for them.
- **Auditory textbooks:** Students who have difficulty reading traditional print texts may use audio-taped texts or texts on CDs to follow along as the text is read aloud. Textbooks on tape or CD are available to students with disabilities through Recordings for the Blind and Dyslexic, as are specialized CD players that allow the student to key in pages, headings or chapters to access specific text quickly. Some even allow the student to insert electronic bookmarks.
- **Talking word processing programs:** Low cost software applications that provide speech output of text displayed on the computer monitor. Some programs highlight the text as it is read.

Spelling

AT is available to support spelling in handwritten and computer generated text.

- **Personal word list or dictionary:** Students maintain a list of commonly misspelled words for personal reference; can be handwritten or computer generated.

- **Hand-held spell checker:** Students type in words and a list of correctly spelled words that closely approximate the misspelled word is provided. Some models offer speech feedback.
- **Word processing program with spell check:** Most word processing programs offer a spell check feature in which misspelled words are underlined.
- **Talking word processing program with spell Check:** These programs are helpful for students who cannot visually identify the correct word on a traditional spell check program. The talking feature allows the student to "listen" for the correct spelling of the word.

Writing

AT to support writing includes a number of low and high tech options.

- **Alternative paper:** For students with fine motor difficulties, modifying the writing paper may be appropriate. One solution is to provide paper with bold lines. Another solution is to use a tactile paper that has a raised line that the student can actually feel. Some students benefit from using graph paper, placing one letter in each box, to improve legibility. Graph paper can also be used for math problems, to assure that the numbers are in alignment.
- **Pencil grips:** This is an inexpensive alternative that gives the student with fine motor difficulties a larger and more supportive means of grasping a pencil.
- **Adapted tape recorder:** Students who have difficulty with writing may be allowed to tape record some of their assignments. Adapted tape recorders can also be used to record class lectures for students who have difficulty taking notes. Tape recorders with an index feature allow the student to mark key points on a tape for later reference
- **Portable word processor:** For students with significant writing difficulties, a portable word processor can provide an alternative to using pencil and paper. These devices use a full size keyboard and allow the student to type in texts. Files can be stored in the device to be uploaded to a computer at a later time. Advantages over a traditional computer or laptop are the economical price, portability, and long battery life.
- **Talking word processor software:** These programs provide feedback by reading aloud what the student has typed in, allowing the student to hear what he has written. This type of multisensory feedback assists the student in identifying and correcting errors.
- **Word prediction software:** This type of software is beneficial for students who have difficulty with spelling and grammar. As the first letter or letters of a word are typed in, the computer predicts the word the student is typing. This type of technology is of benefit to students who type slowly as it reduces the number of keystrokes needed to complete a word.

- **Outlining and webbing software:** This type of software assists students who have difficulty organizing thoughts and planning. Webbing programs allow for graphic diagrams to give the student a visual representation of what is needed to complete the writing task.
- **Voice recognition software:** This type of software has gained in popularity in recent years due to its wide commercial applications. Voice recognition allows the student to "speak" into the computer and the spoken word is translated into written text on the computer screen.

Math

To support students with difficulties in math, both low-tech and high-tech options are available.

- **Calculators**: Students who have difficulty performing math calculations can benefit from the use of a calculator. Adapted calculators may have larger buttons or larger display screens that are useful for students with physical disabilities. Talking calculators are available for students with visual impairments.
- **On-screen electronic worksheets:** For students with physical disabilities who have difficulty with writing, worksheets can be produced in an on-screen format, allowing the student to use a computer screen to answer the questions.
- **Manipulatives of all types:** Students who have difficulty acquiring or retaining math concepts often benefit from objects designed to provide a kinesthetic or visual illustration of the concept. These low tech aids include such things as place value blocks, fraction strips, geared clocks, play money, etc.

AIDS FOR DAILY LIVING

Devices used to assist with self-help skills in activities such as eating, bathing, cooking, dressing, toileting, and home maintenance.

- **Adapted eating utensils:** These are low-tech aids to assist students with feeding themselves. Adapted utensils may include forks, spoons, and knives with an enlarged handles to allow a better grasp or with straps or cuffs for attaching the utensils to the hand for stability. Electronic devices to assist with eating are also available for students with more severe physical disabilities.
- **Adapted drinking aids:** Adaptations to cups and glasses include modified handles or positioning aids to stabilize the cup on a table or wheelchair tray. Some drinking utensils may have tops or modified rims to prevent spillage.
- **Self-care aids:** Students may need assistance to complete self-care tasks such as dressing, grooming, and toileting. Dressing aids include items such as adapted sock aids for putting on and taking off socks, zipper grips for

pulling zippers up and down, no-tie curly laces for shoes, and button hooks to assist in buttoning. Grooming aids include adapted handles on brushes, combs and toothbrushes. Toileting aids could include adapted toilet seats and safety rails for transferring on and off the toilet.

ASSISTIVE LISTENING DEVICES AND ENVIRONMENTAL AIDS

Electronic and non-electronic aids such as amplification devices, closed captioning systems, and environmental alert systems that assist a student with a hearing impairment to access information that is typically presented through an auditory modality.

- **Assistive listening devices:** These devices amplify sound and speech and are appropriate for a student with a hearing impairment. Personal amplification systems are portable and can be used in different environments. These systems consist of a transmitter that transmits the sound to the student's receiving unit. Personal sound field systems consist of a transmitter and a receiver, along with a portable speaker. Sound field systems can also be installed in entire rooms.
- **Text telephones (TTY):** Students with hearing impairments may use the TTY keyboard to type messages over the telephone. Some TTYs have answering machines and some models offer a print out of the text.
- **Closed-captioning devices:** Modern televisions are equipped with closed-captioning options that present the text on the television screen.
- **Environmental aids:** These can include adapted clocks, notification systems, pagers, and warning devices. Visual alert systems may be configured to alert the student of a doorbell, telephone ringing, or smoke detector sounding. Personal pagers may have vibrating and text messaging options.
- **Real-time captioning:** This may be used to caption speech, such as class lectures and presentations to a text display. A computer with specialized software and a projection system are needed for this type of software.

AUGMENTATIVE COMMUNICATION

Electronic and non-electronic devices and software solutions that provide a means for expressive and receptive communication for students with speech and language impairments.

- **Object-based communication displays:** Low-tech solutions that use actual objects to represent daily activities. The student selects or touches the object to communicate a want or need.
- **Picture communication boards and books:** Low-tech solutions that use pictures to represent messages. The pictures are organized according to categories or activities in the student's day.

- **Alphabet boards:** Students who are able to spell, but have limited language, can use an alphabet board to communicate. The student touches the letters to spell out words, phrases, or sentences.
- **Talking switches:** these devices allow for recording of one or two messages. The student activates the switch to "say" the message. A picture may be used in conjunction with the device.
- **Voice output devices (low-tech):** Multiple messages can be recorded on these devices. Messages are recorded and accessed by the student to communicate wants and needs. The low-tech models can range in capacity from one to up to sixty-four messages. Pictures are used on the device as a representative of each message.
- **Voice output devices (middle-tech):** On these devices, the messages are represented by picture symbols. These devices have the capacity to store multiple messages on multiple levels.
- **Voice output devices (high-tech):** High-tech voice output devices are very sophisticated pieces of technology that allow the student to use a computer generated voice to speak for him or her. Some devices uses paper based displays, while others are computer-generated (dynamic) displays. Some offer a keyboard to allow the student to type in messages as well.
- **Integrated communication solutions:** Several software-based applications are available that use a laptop computer in conjunction with a voice output system.

COMPUTER ACCESS AND INSTRUCTION

Input and output devices, alternative access aids, modified or alternative keyboards, switches, special software, and other devices and software solutions that assist a student with a disability to use a computer.

- **Adaptive pointing devices:** Hand-held pointers, hand splints, and mouth sticks can assist the student with physical disabilities to access a computer without the use of hands.
- **Keyboard adaptations:** The computer keyboard can be adapted for students with physical disabilities. Keyguards are devices that cover the computer keyboard and allow access through holes that keep the student from hitting more than one key at a time.
- **Alternative keyboards:** Alternative keyboards may be enlarged for students who need larger targets, or they could be mini-keyboards for students with limited movement.
- **Touch screens:** Touch screens allow access to the computer by touch, rather than by using the keyboard or mouse. This is another area of assistive technology that has shown a lot of growth in recent years, due to the wide commercial usage of touch screen products.

- **On-screen keyboards:** For students who have difficulty using a traditional keyboard, an on-screen keyboard allows the student to write using a mouse, switch, or a scanning system.
- **Mouse alternatives:** Mouse alternatives include trackballs, joysticks, and track pads and are appropriate for students who have difficulty using a traditional mouse.
- **Adaptive output:** Text and graphics on the computer screen can be enlarged for students with visual impairments. Text displayed can also be read aloud by the use of screen reading applications. Printers that print Braille from text typed on the computer are also available for students with visual impairments.

ENVIRONMENTAL CONTROLS

Devices such as switches, environmental control units, and adapted appliances that are used by a student with a physical disability to increase independence. These devices allow the student to use alternate devices, such as switches to control items such as lights, televisions, and door locks.

MOBILITY AIDS

Aids that increase personal mobility, such as wheelchairs, walkers, canes, crutches, and scooters.

PREVOCATIONAL AND VOCATIONAL AIDS

Aids and adaptations that are used to assist a student in completing prevocational and vocational tasks, such as picture-based task analysis sheets, adapted knobs, adapted timers and adapted watches.

RECREATION AND LEISURE AIDS

Aids such as adapted books, switch adapted toys, and leisure computer-based software applications that are used by a student with a disability to increase participation and independence in recreation and leisure activities.

- **Game and puzzle adaptations:** Games and puzzles may be adapted by the addition of knobs to the pieces, by using card holders, and by using grabbing devices to pick up the pieces.
- **Book adaptations:** Adaptations to books may include enlarging the text, providing an audio version to read along, or adding pictures or tactile symbols for non-readers.
- **Switch-adapted toys:** Toys that run on batteries may be adapted to be operated by the use of a switch, thus providing the student with limited physical movement the ability to play with the toy.

SEATING AND POSITIONING

Adaptive seating systems and positioning devices that provide students with appropriate positioning to enhance participation and access to the curriculum. Seating and positioning systems may include seat inserts for wheelchairs, standers, and adaptive chairs, as well as inflated "pillows" or "wiggle seats" for helping children with ADHD remain seated.

VISUAL AIDS

Aids such as magnifiers, talking calculators, Braille writers, adapted tape players, screen reading software applications, and Braille note-taking devices that assist a student with a visual impairment to access and produce information in a print format.

- **Braille writer:** A portable device for producing Braille. Students type in text on the keyboard, using the six key entry method. A copy of the text in Braille is embossed on the paper inserted into the Braille writer.
- **Electronic Braille writer:** An updated version of the Braille writer, the electronic Braille writer is lightweight and offers the option of the text being read aloud to the student. A Braille copy of the text can also be printed out.
- **Closed-circuit television (CCTV):** Assists students with visual impairments by enlarging text and graphics. The page to be read is placed on the base under the camera. The image is displayed on a monitor, with an appropriate level of magnification for the student. Foreground and background colors can be altered for the individual student.
- **Text-enlargement software:** Software is available to increase the size of the text and graphics displayed on the computer monitor.
- **Screen-reading software:** Screen-reading software may also be of benefit to students with visual impairments. These applications allow the computer to read the text aloud.

A student with a disability may require AT in a variety of categories. For example, a student may use an augmentative communication device to supplement communication skills, adaptive switch toys to participate in leisure activities, and an adapted keyboard for accessing software applications on the classroom computer.

AT devices are not limited to specific disability areas. For example, a student with an attention deficit may require an assistive listening device to focus attention on the teacher's voice. Students with various types of disabilities may benefit from audio-recorded materials that were originally developed for students with visual impairments.

The IEP committee determines the need for AT devices and services. Most school districts have policies/procedures regarding AT assessments and have teams of professionals that conduct the evaluation. Often the assessment team will include physical or occupational therapists and speech therapists, to address communication and physical needs. The student's teacher(s) and parents are often included in the AT evaluation. Once it has been determined that an AT device or service is needed, the student's IEP team should document the required device(s) in the IEP.

The use of AT may decrease the amount of other support services a student needs in order to be successful.

In addition to providing the devices, IDEA requires services to support the AT devices. IDEA '97 defines AT Services as: "The term 'assistive technology service' means any service that directly assists a child with a disability in the selection, acquisition, or use of an assistive technology device." There are a variety of services included in this category.

- Evaluation: A functional evaluation of the child's needs in his/her customary environment.
- Acquisition: Whether by purchasing or leasing, the local education agency is required to acquire the device for the student at no cost to the parent.
- Selection and maintenance of the AT device. Included in this area could be the design, fitting, customizing, adapting, repairing, or replacing as needed to support the needs of the child.
- Coordination with other therapies or interventions, including existing education and rehabilitation plans and programs.
- Training or technical assistance for the student, the family, school personnel, employers, or anyone who provides service to the student with a disability.

Suggestions about selecting and using software were given by Male (1994). First, make sure there is a curriculum correspondence between what students are working on at their desks and what they do at the computers, or whatever AT device is in use. This should follow what he calls stages of learning. Then, make certain the students proceed through the five stages of learning. Computer software should be selected with the following stages in mind:

- Acquisition: Introduction of a new skill.
- Proficiency: Practice under supervision to achieve accuracy and speed.
- Maintenance: Continued practice without further instruction.
- Generalization: Application of the new skills in new settings and situations.
- Adaptation: Modifications of the task to meet new needs and demands of varying situations.

COMPUTER-ASSISTED INSTRUCTION

Computers are used to provide a safe, stimulating learning environment for many youth. The computer does not evaluate or offer subjective opinions about the student's work. It merely provides feedback about the correctness or incorrectness of each answer in a series. The computer is like an effective teacher when it:

- Provides immediate attention and feedback
- Individualizes to the particular skill level
- Allows students to work at their own pace
- Makes corrections quickly
- Produces a professional looking product
- Keeps accurate records on correct and error rates
- Ignores inappropriate behavior
- Focuses on the particular response
- Is nonjudgmental (Smith & Luckasson, 1992)

Computers are useful in helping teach traditional academic subjects such as math, reading, spelling, geography, and science. Effective teachers allow for drill and practice on the computer, monitor student progress, and reinforce appropriately. When students have mastered a particular level, these teachers help them progress to another level. Reasoning and problem-solving are other skill areas that teachers have discovered can be taught using computers.

One type of newly developed computer software is the program Hypertext. It enables further explanation of textbook material. The explanation is accessed by a simple press of a key while the student is working on the learning material. For example, by pressing a single key, students can access definitions of difficult vocabulary words, reworded complicated text, additional detailed maps, and further information about concepts being introduced in the text. By using this program, teachers can help students by creating individualized lessons. Students with learning disabilities especially benefit.

Computer games can enhance learning skills and provide a highly desired reinforcement opportunity. When played alone, the games serve as leisure activities for the individual. When played with classmates, the games can help develop interpersonal relationships. Use of computer games is particularly applicable to youngsters with behavioral disorders and learning and intellectual disabilities, as well as those without any identified disability.

DOMAIN IV   WORKING IN A PROFESSIONAL ENVIRONMENT

COMPETENCY 007   UNDERSTAND THE HISTORICAL, PHILOSOPHICAL, AND LEGAL FOUNDATIONS OF THE FIELD OF SPECIAL EDUCATION

Skill 7.1   **Demonstrating knowledge of the historical and philosophical foundations of special education and contemporary issues pertaining to the education of individuals with disabilities, including the roles and organizational structures of general and special education and the parts they play in providing total services to all students**

SIGNIFICANT SUPREME COURT CASES INVOLVING INTERPRETATION OF IDEA

Following the passage of P.L. 94-142 and IDEA, questions have arisen over the interpretation of *least restrictive environment* and *free, appropriate public education.* The courts have been asked to judge the extent of a school district's obligation to provide support services and suspension procedures for students with disabilities. A brief description of some of the cases that the U.S. Supreme Court reviewed and the rulings are included in this section. These cases have addressed such issues as least restrictive environment, free and appropriate public education, transportation, suspension of exceptional education students, and provision of services in a private school setting.

Board of Education v. Rowley, 1982

This case concerned the interpretation of "Free and Public Education," and the lengths to which schools are required to go in order to provide it. Amy Rowley was a deaf elementary school student whose parents rejected their school district's proposal to provide a tutor and speech therapist services to supplement their daughter's instruction in the regular classroom. Her parents insisted on an interpreter, even though Amy was making satisfactory social, academic, and educational progress without one. They argued that although she was progressing well, there was a serious discrepancy between her level of achievement and her potential without the handicap. They held that the absence of an interpreter prevented her from reaching her full potential. In deciding in favor of the school district, the Supreme Court confirmed the Act's requirement of a "basic floor of opportunity consistent with equal protection," but stated that this "basic floor" did not require "anything more than equal access." It explicitly ruled that schools are **not** required to 'maximize the potential of handicapped children 'commensurate with the opportunity provided to other children.' It further ruled that "if the child is being educated in the regular classrooms of the public education system, (services) should be reasonably calculated to enable the child to achieve passing marks and advance from grade to grade." Finally, the Court ruled that Amy did not need an interpreter, because "evidence firmly establishes that Amy is receiving an `adequate' education, since she performs better than the average child in her class and is advancing easily from grade to grade."

Irving Independent School District v. Tatro, 1984

IDEA lists health services as one of the related services that schools are mandated to provide to exceptional students. Amber Tatro, who had spina bifida, required the insertion of a catheter on a regular schedule in order to empty her bladder. The issue was specifically over the classification of clean, intermittent catheterization (CIC) as a medical service (not covered under IDEA) or a related health service, which would be covered. In this instance, the catheterization was not declared a medical service, but a related service necessary for the student to have in order to benefit from special education. The school district was obliged to provide the service. The Tatro case has implications for students with other medical impairments who may need services to allow them to attend classes at the school.

Smith v. Robinson, 1984

This case concerned reimbursement of attorney's fees for parents who win litigation under IDEA. At the time of this case, IDEA did not provide for such reimbursement. Following this ruling, Congress passed a law awarding attorney's fees to parents who win their litigation.

Honig v. Doe, 1988

Essentially, students may not be denied education or be excluded from school when their misbehavior is related to their handicap. The *stay put* provision of IDEA allows students to remain in their current educational setting pending the outcome of administrative or judicial hearings. In the case of behavior that is a danger to the student or others, the court allows school districts to apply their normal procedures for dealing with dangerous behavior, such as time-out, loss of privileges, detention, or study carrels. Where the student has presented an immediate threat to others, that student may be temporarily suspended for up to 10 school days to give the school and the parents time to review the IEP and discuss possible alternatives to the current placement.

Oberti vs. Board of Education of the Borough of Clementon School District, 1993

It was determined that IDEA requires school systems to supplement and realign their resources to move beyond those systems, structures, and practices that tend to result in unnecessary segregation of children with disabilities.
The Act does *not* require states to offer *the same* educational experience to a child with disabilities as is generally provided for children without disabilities. To the contrary, states must address the unique needs of a disabled child, recognizing that

that child may benefit differently from education in the regular classroom than other students. In summary, the fact that a child with disabilities will learn differently from his or her education within a regular classroom does not justify exclusion from that environment.

TEACHER ADVOCACY FOR STUDENTS AND FAMILIES

Learning about one's self involves identifying learning styles, strengths and weakness, interests, and preferences. For students with mild disabilities, developing an awareness of the accommodations they need will help them ask for necessary accommodations on a job and in postsecondary education. Students can also help identify alternative ways they can learn.

Self-advocacy involves effectively communicating one's own rights, needs, and desires and taking responsibility for making decisions that have an impact on one's life.

Developing self-advocacy skills in students who are involved in the transition process requires many elements. Helping the student to identify future goals or desired outcomes in transition planning areas is a good place to start. Self-knowledge is critical for the student in determining the direction that transition planning will take.

The role of the teacher in promoting self-advocacy should include encouraging the student to participate in the IEP process and other key parts of their educational development. Self-advocacy issues and lessons are effective when they are incorporated into the student's daily life. Teachers should listen to the student's problems and ask the student for input on possible changes that he or she may need. The teacher should talk with the student about possible solutions, discussing the pros and cons of certain actions. A student who self-advocates should feel supported and encouraged. Good self-advocates know how to ask questions and get help from other people. They do not let other people do everything for them. Students need to practice newly acquired self-advocacy skills. Teachers should have students role play various situations, such as setting up a class schedule, moving out of the home, and asking for accommodations needed for a course.

The impact of transition planning on a student with a disability is very great. The student should be an active member of the transition team and the focus of all activities. Students often think that being passive and relying on others to take care of them is the way to get action. Students should be encouraged to express their opinions throughout the transition process. They need to learn how to express themselves so that others listen and take them seriously. These skills should be practiced within a supportive and caring environment.

ROLE OF THE FAMILY

The discovery at birth or initial diagnosis of a child's disabling condition(s) has a strong impact upon the family unit. Though reactions are unique to individuals, the first emotion generally felt by the parent of a child with disabilities is shock, followed by disbelief, guilt, rejection, shame, denial, and helplessness. As parents finally accept the reality of their child's condition, many report feelings of anxiety or fearfulness about their personal ability to care for and rear an exceptional child. Many parents will doctor shop, hoping to find answers, while others will reject or deny information given them by health care professionals.

The presence of a child with a disability within the family unit creates changes and possible stresses that will need addressing. Many will feel parenting demands greatly in excess of a nondisabled child's requirements. "A child (with a disability) frequently needs more time, energy, attention, patience, and money than the child (without a disability), and frequently returns less success, achievement, parent pride-inducing behavior, privacy, feelings of security and well-being" (Paul, 1981, p.6).

The family as a microcosmic unit in a society plays a vital role in many ways. The family assumes a protective and nurturing function, is the primary unit for social control, and plays a major role in the transmission of cultural values and mores. This role is enacted concurrently with changes in our social system at large.

Paradoxically, the parents who were formerly viewed as the cause of their children's disability are now expected to enact positive changes in their children's lives.

Siblings play an important role in fostering the social and emotional developments of a brother or sister with a disability. A wide range of feelings and reactions will evolve as siblings interact. Some experience guilt over being the normal child and try to overcompensate by being the successful, perfect child for their parents. Others react in a hostile, resentful manner toward the amount of time and care the disabled sibling receives, and frequently create disruption as a way of obtaining parental attention.

The extended family, especially grandparents, can provide support and assistance to the nuclear family unit if they live within a manageable proximity; childcare services for an evening or a few days can provide a means of reprieve for heavily involved parents.

PARENTS AS ADVOCATES AND PARTNERS

Ironically, the possibility for establishing the partnership, which is now sought by educators with parents of children with disabilities, came about largely through the advocacy efforts of parents. The state compulsory education laws began in 1918 and were adopted across the nation with small variances in agricultural regions. However, because these children did not fit in with the general school curriculum, most continued to be turned away at the schoolhouse door, leaving the custodial services at state or private institutions as the primary alternative placement site for parents.

Educational policies reflected the litigation and legislation of the times, which overwhelmingly sided with the educational system and not with the family. After all, the educational policies reflected the prevailing philosophies of the times, such as Social Darwinism (i.e., survival of the fittest). Thus, persons with disabilities were set apart from the rest of society—literally out of sight, out of mind. Those with severe disabilities were placed in institutions, and those with moderate disabilities were kept at home to do family or farm chores.

Following the two world wars, the realization that disabling conditions could be incurred by a member of any family came to the forefront. Several celebrity families allowed stories to be published in national magazines about a family member with an identified disability, thus taking the entire plight of this family syndrome out of the closet.

The 1950s brought about the founding of many parent and professional organizations, and the movement continued into the next decade. Learning groups included the *National Association of Parents and Friends of Mentally Retarded Children* founded in 1950 and later called the *National Association for Retarded Children*, and now named the *National Association of Retarded Citizens*; the *International Parents Organization* in 1957, as the parents' branch of the *Alexander Graham Bell Association for Parents of the Deaf* in 1965. *The Epilepsy Foundation of America* was founded in 1967. *The International Council for Exceptional Children* had been established by faculty and students at Columbia University as early as 1922, and the *Council for Exceptional Children* recognized small parent organizations in the late 1940s.

During the 1950s, Public Law 85-926 brought about support for preparing teachers to work with children with disabilities so that these children might receive educational services.

The 1960s was the first period during which parents received tangible support from the executive branch of the national government. In 1960, the *White House Conference on Children and Youth* declared that a child should only be separated from his family as a last resort. This declaration gave vital support to parents' efforts toward securing a public education for their youngsters with disabilities. Parent groups are a major component in assuring appropriate services for children with disabilities. They are coequal with special education and community service agencies. Their role is individual and political advocacy and socio-psychological support. Great advances in services for children with disabilities have been made through the efforts of parent advocacy groups, which have been formed to represent almost every type of disabling condition.

PUBLIC ATTITUDES TOWARD INDIVIDUALS WITH DISABILITIES

Although the origin of special education services for youngsters with disabilities is relatively recent, the history of public attitude toward people with disabling conditions was recorded as early as the civilizations of ancient Greece and Rome. The Spartans practiced infanticide, the killing or abandonment of malformed or sickly babies. The ancient Greeks and Romans thought people with disabilities were cursed and forced them to beg for food and shelter. Those who could not fend for themselves were allowed to perish. Some with mental disabilities were employed as fools for the entertainment of the Roman royalty.

In the time of Christ, society thought that people with disabilities were suffering the punishment of God. Those with emotional disturbances were possessed by the devil, and, although early Christianity advocated humane treatment of those who were not normal physically or mentally, many remained outcasts of society, sometimes pitied and sometimes scorned.

During the Middle Ages, persons with disabilities were viewed within the aura of the unknown and were treated with a mixture of fear and reverence. Some were wandering beggars, while others were used as jesters in the courts. The Reformation, however, brought about a change of attitude. Individuals with disabilities were accused of being possessed by the devil, and exorcism flourished. Many innocent people were put in chains and cast into dungeons.

The early seventeenth century was marked by a softening of public attitude toward persons with disabilities. Hospitals began to provide treatment for those with emotional disturbances and mental retardation. A manual alphabet for those with deafness was developed, and John Locke became the first person to differentiate between persons who were mentally retarded and those who were emotionally disturbed.

In America, however, the colonists treated people with severe mental disorders as criminals, while those who were harmless were left to beg or were treated as paupers. At one time, it was common practice to sell them to the person who would provide for them at the least cost to the public. When this practice was stopped, persons with mental retardation were put into poorhouses, where conditions were often extremely squalid.

The Nineteenth Century: The Beginning of Training

In 1799, Jean Marc Itard, a French physician, found a 12-year old boy who had been abandoned in the woods of Averyron, France. His attempts to civilize and educate the boy, Victor, established many of the educational principles presently in use in the field of special education, including developmental and multi-sensory approaches, sequencing of tasks, individualized instruction, and a curriculum geared toward functional life skills.

Itard's work had an enormous impact upon public attitude toward individuals with disabilities. They began to be seen as educable. During the late 1700s, experts devised rudimentary procedures that could be used to teach those with sensory impairments (i.e., deaf, blind). This event was closely followed in the early 1800s by attempts to teach students with mild intellectual disabilities and emotional disorders (i.e., at that time referred to as the "idiotic" and "insane").

Throughout Europe, societies build schools for students with visual and hearing impairments, paralleled by the founding of similar institutions in the United States. In 1817, Thomas Hopkins Gallaudet founded the first American school for students who were deaf, known today as Gallaudet College in Washington, D.C., one of the world's best institutions of higher learning for those with deafness. Gallaudet's work was followed closely by that of Samuel Gridley who was instrumental in founding the Perkins Institute for blind students in 1829.

The mid-1800s saw the further development of Itard's philosophy of education of students with mental disabilities. Around that time, his student, Edward Seguin, immigrated to the United States, where he established his philosophy of education for persons with mental retardation in a publication entitle *Idiocy and Its Treatment by the Physiological Method* in 1866. Seguin was instrumental in establishing the first residential school for individuals with retardation in the United States.

State legislatures began to assume responsibility for housing people with physical and mental disabilities. This institutional care was largely custodial. Institutions were often referred to as warehouses because of the deplorable conditions. Humanitarians such as Dorothea Dix helped relieve anguish and suffering in institutions for persons with mental illnesses.

1900–1919: Specific Programs

The early twentieth century saw the publication of the first standardized test of intelligence by Alfred Binet of France. The test was designed to identify educationally substandard children, but by 1916, the test was revised by the American Louis Terman, and the concept of the intelligence quotient (IQ) was introduced. Since then, the IQ test has come to be used as a predictor of both retarded (delayed) and advanced intellectual development.

At approximately the same time, Italian physician Maria Montessori was concerned with the development of effective techniques for early childhood education. Although she is known primarily for her contributions to this field, her work included methods of education for children with mental retardation, and the approach she developed is used in preschool programs today.

Ironically, the advancement of science and the scientific method led special education to its worst setback in modern times. In 1912, psychologist Henry Goddard published a study based on the Killikak family, in which he traced five generations of the descendants of a man who had one legitimate child and one illegitimate child. Among the descendants of the legitimate child were numerous mental defectives and social deviates. From this information, Goddard concluded that mental retardation and social deviation were inherited traits, and, therefore, mental and social deviates were a threat to society, an observation that he called the Eugenics Theory. Reinforcing the concept of retardation as hereditary deviance was a popular philosophy called *Positivism*, under which these unscientific conclusions were believed to be fixed, mechanical laws that were carrying mankind to inevitable improvement. Falling by the wayside was seen as the natural, scientific outcome for the defective person in society. Consequently, during this time, mass institutionalization and sterilization of persons with mental retardation and criminals were practiced.

Nevertheless, public school programs for persons with retardation gradually increased during this same period. Furthermore, the first college programs for preparing Special Education Teachers were established between 1900 and 1920.

1919–1949: Professional Personnel and Expansion of Services

As awareness of the need for medical and mental health treatment in the community was evidenced during the 1920s, halfway houses became a means for monitoring the transition from institution to community living. Outpatient clinics were established to provide increased medical care. Social workers and other support personnel were dispensed into the community to coordinate services for the needy. The thrust toward humane treatment within the community came to an abrupt halt during the 1930s and 1940s, primarily because of economic depression and widespread dissatisfaction toward the recently enacted social programs.

Two factors related to the World Wars I and II helped improve public opinion toward persons with disabilities. The first factor was the intensive screening of the population of young men with physical and mental disabilities that were in the United States. Second, patriotism caused people to regard the enormous number of young men who returned from the wars with physical and emotional disabilities in a different light than they would have been regarded before that time. People became more sensitive to the problems of the veterans with disabilities, and this acceptance generalized to other groups in the population with special needs.

With increased public concern for people with disabilities came new research. John B. Watson introduced behaviorism, which shifted the treatment emphasis from psychoanalysis to learned behavior. He demonstrated in 1920 that Albert, an 11-month old boy, learned maladaptive (or abnormal) behavior through conditioning. B.F. Skinner followed with a book entitled the *Behavior of Organisms,* which outlined principles of operant (voluntary) behavior.

In 1922, the Council for Exceptional Children (first called the International Council for Exceptional Children) was founded. During the 1920s, many comprehensive statewide programs were initiated. The number of special education programs in public schools increased at a rapid rate until the 1930s, when the push for humane and effective treatment of people with disabilities began to diminish once again. The period of the Depression was marked by large-scale institutionalization and lack of treatment. Part of the cause was inadequately planned programs and poorly trained teachers. World War II did much to swing the pendulum back in the other direction, however, and inaugurated the most active period in the history of the development of special education.

1950–1969: The Parents, the Legislators, and the Courts Become Involved

The first two decades of the second half of this century were characterized by increased federal involvement in general education, gradually extending to special education. In 1950, came the establishment of the National Association of Retarded Children, later renamed the National Association of Retarded Citizens (NARC). It was the result of the efforts among concerned parents who felt the need for an appropriate public education. Increased media coverage exposed the miserable conditions in some of the institutions devoted to caring for people with disabilities, especially those with intellectual and emotional disabilities, and treatment consequently became more humane.

At about this time, parents of children with disabilities discovered the federal courts as a powerful agent on behalf of their children. The 1954 decision in the Brown v. the Topeka Board of Education case guaranteed equal opportunity rights to a free public education for all citizens, and the parents of children and youth with disabilities insisted that their children be included in that decision.

From this point on, the court cases and public laws enacted as a result of court decisions are too numerous to include in their entirety. Only those few that had the greatest impact on the development of special education as we know it today are listed. Collectively, they are part of a movement in U.S. Supreme Court history known as the Doctrine of Selective Incorporation, under which the states are compelled to honor various substantive rights under procedural authority of the 14th Amendment.

Continuous passing of legislation, community agency involvement, and the media have brought individuals with disabilities increased social acceptance and awareness.

Cultural and Community Influences on Public Attitudes toward Individuals with Disabilities

While society has progressed and many ideas are acceptable today that were not acceptable yesterday, having a disability still carries a stigma. Historically, people with disabilities have been ostracized from their communities. Large numbers of people with special needs were institutionalized at birth because the relatives did not know what to do, they felt embarrassed to admit they had a child with a disability, or they gave in to the cultural peer pressure to put their "problem" away. Sometimes this fear meant hiding a child's disability, which may even have led to locking a child in a room in the house. Perhaps the worst viewpoint society expressed before the 1970s and one that still prevails today is that the person with special needs cannot contribute to society.

Today, American society has exchanged the "must institutionalize" method for a "normalize" concept. Advocates have purchased houses in local communities and, in these houses, provide supervision or nursing care that allows people with disabilities to have "normal" social living arrangements. Congress passed laws that have given those with disabilities access public facilities. American society has widened doorways, added special bathrooms, etc. The regular education classroom teacher is now learning to accept and teach students with special needs. America's film industry today rarely produces a movie or TV show without including someone with special needs. The concept of acceptance appears to be developing for those with physically noticeable handicaps.

But, those with special needs who appear in such media as television and movies generally are those who rise above their label as disabled because of an extraordinary skill. Most people in the community are portrayed as accepting the disabled person when that special skill is noted. In addition, those who continue to express revulsion or prejudice towards the person with a disability often express remorse when the special skill is noted or peer pressure becomes too intense. This portrayal often ignores those who appear normal by appearance but who have learning and emotional disabilities and who often feel and suffer from the prejudices

The most significant group any individual faces is the peer group. Pressure to appear normal and not "needy" in any area is intense from early childhood to adulthood. During the teen years when young people are beginning to express their individuality, the very appearance of walking into a special education classroom often brings feelings of inadequacy and labeling by peers that the student is "special." Being considered normal is the desire of all individuals with disabilities regardless of the age or disability. People with disabilities today, as they did many years ago, measure their successes by how their achievements mask their disabilities.

The most difficult cultural and community outlook on those who are disabled comes in the adult work world where disabilities of persons can become highly evident and often cause difficulty in finding work and keeping their jobs. This place is particularly difficult for those who have not learned to self-advocate or accommodate for their special needs.

Interagency agreements

States such as California and Texas have implemented laws to govern and require cooperation among required services to best serve the parents and children with special needs. California's law (AB3632) goes a step beyond requiring cooperation of needed departmental resources such as Education, Health Services, Social Services, and Rehabilitation Services. It requires a sharing of information, personnel, and financial resources to provide a focused delivery that best meets the person's needs.

Nongovernmental agencies often may deliver and coordinate such agreements and often involve additional community resources for the student and their family. The stated purposes of interagency agreements is to provide the best services to a person with a disability so that they may receive an education that prepares them for living and working in an integrated community setting of their choice. These services may coordinate delivery of services in both the home and school environment.

Special education teachers may need to inform the parents of their students about interagency agreements and the benefits of case managers so that they may better advocate for their children.

Deinstitutionalization and community based placements

The deinstitutionalization movement occurred simultaneously with efforts to treat individuals in their least restrictive environment. For many formerly institutionalized persons, semi-protected community settings could accommodate their needs. Another term, *normalization*, was coined when efforts were made for persons with disabilities to live their lives as close to the family setting as possible. Movement toward less restrictive environments culminated in establishing halfway residential houses, community residences (i.e., community group homes, foster family homes, apartment living), rehabilitation facilities, sheltered workshops, and vocational training programs.

The formation of local agencies and foundations assisted in the rehabilitation of these formerly institutionalized individuals. Services provided by these programs may differ somewhat from one locality to another; however, there are enough similarities that generalities can be stated.

Rehabilitation facilities and sheltered workshops are particularly appropriate for individuals with severe disabilities. These facilities are geared toward slower-paced, intensive instruction in an effort to develop effective work habits, occupational skills, appropriate personal-social skills, and vocational interests. Some students can later receive vocational technical or on-the-job training in the community. In addition, these facilities are considered both a treatment and a training medium and generally have a variety of professionally trained counselors, evaluators, teachers, and supervisors. Sheltered workshops may provide employment for persons who can work productively in a protective, semi-competitive environment for at least a short period of time. These individuals would not be as likely to find successful experiences in a less restrictive, more competitive work setting.

Halfway residential houses are available in some communities for formerly institutionalized individuals who need support or supervision while receiving vocational training and other career development services elsewhere. Some of these facilities provide daily living and personal-social instruction, particularly if they are affiliated with a rehabilitative or sheltered workshop. A small staff may be available for individual and group counseling.

In some communities group homes have been established that operate as much on the family concept as possible. The group home creates an environment that is more like family living than that of a large institution. It also provides a setting in which the variety of skills necessary for effective living can be pursued. Another type of alternative living unit is that of foster family homes. Most foster family arrangements are regulated by state and municipal licensing boards. In most cases, foster parents receive fees, but they do not usually receive training. Supervision of foster care homes is generally less rigorous than it is for group homes.

Apartment living arrangements, though not as prevalent or widely accepted at the present time as the group home concept, are rapidly gaining momentum. In this newer semi-independent living concept, the supervisor may live with the client, or clients may live together in a cluster of apartments in a separate part of the same building as the supervisor. As skills considered necessary for independent living are acquired and self-sufficiency is exhibited, clients are encouraged to move into apartments of their own. Periodic visits are made by supervisors to assure that the necessary level of self-care is maintained. The majority of clients who live in this type of arrangement attend a training program that helps them develop vocational and independent living skills. These clients remain a part of life-care and counseling programs but have work and leisure activities apart from agency staff supervising their living units.

INCLUSION

Inclusion is both a concept and a method of service delivery. It includes both indirect and direct services rendered by the special education teacher. With indirect services, the special education teacher consults with the regular classroom teacher about the type of instruction and instructional materials that would best meet the needs of a particular student. Through direct services, the special education teacher comes into the regular classroom and team-teaches with the general education teacher. The special education teacher works with individuals, small groups, and large groups of students who are experiencing similar educational difficulties.

Composite Scenario of an Inclusive Educational Setting

The following composite scenario provides a brief description of how regular and special teachers work together to address the individual needs of all of their students (ERIC Clearinghouse on Disabilities and Gifted Education, 1993).

Jane Smith teaches third grade at Lincoln Elementary School. Three days a week, she co-teaches the class with Lynn Vogel, a special education teacher. Their twenty-five students include four who have special needs because of disabilities and two others who currently need special help in specific curriculum areas. Each of the students with a disability has an IEP that was developed by a team that included both teachers. The teachers, paraprofessionals, and the school principal believe that these students have a great deal to contribute to the class and that they will achieve their best in the environment of a general education classroom.

All of the school personnel have attended in-service training designed to develop collaborative skills for teaming and problem solving. Mrs. Smith and the two professionals who work in the classroom also received special training on disabilities and how to create an inclusive classroom environment. The school's principal, Ben Parks, worked in special education many years ago and has received training on the impact of new special education developments and instructional arrangements on school administration. Each year, Mr. Parks works with the building staff to identify areas in which new training is needed. For specific questions that may arise, technical assistance is available through a regional special education cooperative.

Mrs. Smith and Miss Vogel share responsibility for teaching and supervising their paraprofessional. In addition to the time they spend together in the classroom, they spend two hours each week planning instruction, plus additional planning time with other teachers and support personnel who work with their students.

The teachers use their joint planning time to problem-solve and discuss the use of special instructional techniques for all students who need special assistance. Monitoring and adapting instruction for individual students is an ongoing activity. The teachers use curriculum-based measurement in systematically assessing their students' learning progress. They adapt curricula so that lessons begin at the edge of the students' knowledge, adding new material at the students' pace, and presenting it in a style consistent with the students' learning style. For some students, pre-organizers or chapter previews are used to bring out the most important points of the material to be learned; for other students new vocabulary words may need to be highlighted or reduced reading levels may be required. Some students may use special activity worksheets, while others may learn best by using audiocassettes.

In the classroom, the teachers group students differently for different activities. Sometimes, the teachers and paraprofessionals divide the class, each teaching a small group or tutoring individuals. They use cooperative learning projects to help the students learn to work together and to develop social relationships. Peer tutors provide extra help to students who need it. Students without disabilities are more than willing to help their friends' who have disabilities and vice versa.

While the regular classroom may not be the best learning environment for every child with a disability, it is highly desirable for all who can benefit. It provides contact with age-peers and prepares all students for the diversity of the world beyond the classroom.

Successful Inclusion

The following are activities and support systems that are commonly found where successful inclusion has occurred.

Attitudes and beliefs

- The regular teacher believes that the student can succeed.
- The school personnel are committed to accepting responsibility for the learning outcomes of students with disabilities.
- School personnel and the students in the class have been prepared to receive a student with disabilities.

Services and physical accommodation

- Services needed by the student are available (e.g., health, physical, occupational, or speech therapy).
- Adequate numbers of personnel, including aides and support personnel, are available.
- Adequate staff development and technical assistance, based on the needs of the school personnel, are provided (e.g., information on disabilities, instructional methods, awareness and acceptance activities for students, and team-building skills).
- Appropriate policies and procedures for monitoring individual students' progress, including grading and testing, are in place.

Collaboration

- Special educators are part of the instructional or planning team.
- Teaming approaches are used for problem solving and program implementation.
- Regular teachers, special education teachers, and other specialists collaborate (e.g., co-teach, team teach, work together on teacher assistance teams).

Instructional materials

- Teachers have the knowledge and skills needed to select and adapt curricula and instructional methods according to individual student needs.
- A variety of instructional arrangements is available (e.g., team teaching, cross-grade grouping, peer tutoring, and teacher assistance teams).
- Teachers foster a cooperative learning environment and promote socialization.

Application of technology

The reauthorization of IDEA 2004 provided funding to expand the use of technology in the IEP process. IDEA also provided funding to improve the use of technology by children with disabilities in the classroom, and it supported the use of technology with universal design principles and assistive technology devices to maximize accessibility to the general education curriculum for children with disabilities.

Each public agency must make sure that assistive technology devices or services are available to children with disabilities if needed as a part of the child's special education, related services, or supplementary aids and services. On a case-by-case basis, the use of school-purchased assistive technology devices in a child's home or in other settings is required if the child's IEP team determines that the child needs access to those devices in order to receive a free appropriate public education (FAPE).

Before the passing of IDEA 2004, *the Assistive Technology Act of 1998* was passed to provide financial assistance to states so that they could maintain a permanent comprehensive statewide program of technology-related assistance, for individuals with disabilities. It was designed to increase the availability and funding for assistive technology devices and services. In addition, its goals were to:

- Increase the involvement of individuals with disabilities and their family members in decisions related to the provision of assistive technology devices and services
- Increase the awareness of laws that facilitate the availability of assistive technology devices and services
- Facilitate the change of laws to obtain increased availability or provision of assistive technology devices and services
- Increase the likelihood that individuals with disabilities will be able to obtain and maintain possession of assistive technology devices

Skill 7.2 **Applying knowledge of the legal bases and ethical guidelines pertaining to the education of students with disabilities (e.g., rights and responsibilities of students, parents/guardians, teachers, and schools; due process and procedural safeguards; data privacy requirements; assessment procedures; guidelines related to behavior management)**

SCHOOL AND EDUCATOR RESPONSIBILITIES

IDEA legislation is legally binding on all educators and schools and, in its current form, requires the following:

1. **Free Appropriate Public Education (FAPE)**
   This includes special education and related services which: (1) are provided at public expense; (2) meet the standards of the state educational agency; (3) include preschool, elementary, and/or secondary education in the state involved, and (4) are provided in conformity with each student's individualized education program, if the program is developed to meet requirements of the law.

   IDEA 2004 revised the definition of FAPE by mandating that students have maximum access to appropriate general education. Additionally, LRE placement for those students with disabilities must have the same school placement rights as those students who are not disabled. IDEA 2004 recognizes that due to the nature of some disabilities, appropriate education might vary in the amount of participation in the general education setting. For some students, FAPE will mean a choice of the type of educational institution they attend (for example, a public or a private school), any of which must provide the special education services deemed necessary for the student through the IEP.

2. **Notification and procedural rights for parents**
   These include:
   - The right to examine records and obtain independent evaluations
   - The right to receive a clearly written notice (in their native language) that states the results of the school's evaluation of their child and whether the child meets eligibility requirements for placement or continuation of special services, as well as advance notices of CSE meetings
   - Parents who disagree with the school's decision may request a *due process* hearing and a *judicial hearing* if they do not receive satisfaction through due process.

3. **Identification and services to all children**
   States must conduct public outreach programs to seek out and identify children who might need services. Often referred to as *Zero Reject*, this requirement means schools cannot reject students regardless of the type

(e.g., retardation, contagious disease) or severity of a disability, but must serve ALL. Efforts to find and serve all must be reported annually.

4. Necessary related services

Developmental, corrective, and other support services that make it possible for a student to benefit from special education services must be provided. These might include speech, recreation, or physical therapy.

5. Individualized assessments

Evaluations and tests must be nondiscriminatory, individualized, and in the student's native language. IDEA 97 also placed an additional requirement of a definitive reason why a standard general education assessment would not be deemed appropriate for a child and how the child should then be assessed.

6. Individualized Education Plans

Each student receiving special education services must have an *Individualized Education Plan* developed at a meeting that is attended by a qualified representative of the local education agency (LEA). Others who should attend include the proposed special education teachers, mainstream teachers, parents, and, when appropriate, the student.

7. Least Restrictive Environment (LRE)

There is no simple definition of LRE. LRE differs with the child's needs. LRE means that the student is placed in an environment that is not dangerous, overly controlling, or intrusive but that is as close to the general education setting as is consistent with the child's needs. The student should be given opportunities to experience what peers of similar mental or chronological age are doing. IDEA recognizes that LRE for one child might be a regular classroom with support services, while LRE for another might be a self-contained classroom in a special school.

IDEA requires schools to establish performance goals and indicators for children with disabilities—consistent to the maximum extent appropriate with other goals and standards for all children established by the state—and to report on progress toward meeting those goals.

In summary, all schools, teachers, and other school personnel providing services to students with disabilities are required by law to abide by the provisions of each child's IEP.

CONSEQUENCES FOR VIOLATING IDEA (AND IEP) PROVISIONS

Any school system, school, or teacher violating IDEA law can be held legally accountable. "Violating IDEA" can mean many different things. School systems can be found in violation if they fail to adequately search for students with disabilities, if they take too long to identify and provide services to a child, or if they fail to provide services listed in the IEP, among other things. *When teachers are found in violation, it is usually because they have failed to provide the modifications and accommodations required by a student's IEP.* All such "violations" mean, basically, that a student's rights have been violated, that something a school or teacher did or did NOT do deprived a student of the right to FAPE or LRE.

Katsyannis and Maag (1997) found that "Courts have consistently upheld the right of parents to receive relief for violations that inhibit a student's right to FAPE" (p. 452). This usually involves compensatory education at the expense of the school, reimbursement to the family of educational costs and legal fees, paying for alternative schools and services, and, increasingly, awarding monetary damages to students and their families. These damages have been assessed against schools and *against individual teachers.* In Doe v. Withers (1992), for instance, the school was assessed a large fine and the teacher involved was required to pay $35,000.00 in restitution to the parents.

Such legal requirements and the potential consequences for violations can pose a challenge to the teachers who must be familiar with each child's IEP and provide the modifications and accommodations outlined in it. The teacher who is listed as the liaison on the IEP is also responsible for keeping an eye on everyone *else* providing services to the student to be sure *they* are following the IEP. If the IEP says, for example, that the student may dictate answers to tests, the teacher cannot say that there is no time for this or no aide to help. If the IEP says to enlarge printed materials and place information on four separate panels with a frame around each, the teacher cannot plead a lack of ink or paper. If the IEP says the child gets a ten minute break every hour, the teacher must find a way to deliver the lessons in the remaining fifty minutes.

These requirements can be challenging, but teachers must understand that they are legally required to follow them. IDEA is the blueprint for special education today and it is the teacher's responsibility to be familiar with it in its most current form and to abide by its provisions. It may not always be easy, but it's part of the job.

Additional Parental Rights

Parents and students have certain rights under the No Child Left Behind (NCLB) Act of 2002. The purpose of the NCLB is to ensure that all children have a fair, equal, and significant opportunity to obtain a high-quality education. The act has several parental involvement provisions that reflect shared accountability between schools and parents for high student achievement, including expanded public school choice and supplemental educational services for eligible children in low performing schools, local development of parental involvement plans with sufficient flexibility to address local needs, and the building of parents' capacities for using effective practices to improve their own children's academic achievement.

Great Resource: Printable Parents' Rights Guides:
http://www.specialednews.com/behavior/behavnews/CECbehavassess021900.html

CONFIDENTIALITY

The Family Educational Rights and Privacy Act (1974), also known as the Buckley Amendment, assures confidentiality of student records. Parents are afforded the right to examine, review, and request changes in information deemed inaccurate and stipulate persons who might access their child's records.

INFORMED CONSENT

Parents must give written consent prior to the first comprehensive evaluation of their child for eligibility for special services. They must also consent to re-evaluations. If services are to be initiated or eliminated outside of a formal IEP meeting, parental consent is required. If, however, a parent ignores requests for feedback, some changes in the child's services can be made without parental consent. For this reason, it is important that parents understand when their consent is required and when it is not required. Such issues are generally covered in a parents' rights brochure given to parents during the pre-referral or referral process.

DUE PROCESS

"Due process is a set of procedures designed to ensure the fairness of educational decisions and the accountability of both professionals and parents in making these decisions" (Kirk and Gallagher, 1986, p. 24). These procedures serve as a mechanism by which the child and his or her family can voice their opinions, concerns, or even dissents. Due process safeguards exist in all matters pertaining to identification, evaluation, and educational placement.

Due process occurs in two realms: substantive and procedural. Substantive due process is the content of the law (e.g., appropriate placement for special education students). Procedural due process is the form through which substantive due process is carried out (e.g., parental permission for testing). IDEA contains many items of both substantive and procedural due process, such as:

1. A due process hearing may be initiated by parents or the Local Education Agency (LEA) as an impartial forum for challenging decisions about identification, evaluation, or placement. Either party may present evidence, cross-examine witnesses, obtain a record of the hearing, and be advised by counsel or by individuals having expertise in the education of individuals with disabilities. Findings may be appealed to the state education agency (SEA), and, if still dissatisfied, either party may bring civil action in a state or federal district court. Hearing timelines are set by legislation.
2. Parents may obtain an independent evaluation if there is disagreement about the education evaluation performed by the LEA. The results of such an

evaluation: (1) must be considered in any decision made with respect to the provision of a free, appropriate public education for the child and (2) may be presented as evidence at a hearing. Further, the parents may request this evaluation at public expense: (1) if a hearing officer requests an independent educational evaluation or (2) if the decision from a due process hearing is that the LEA's evaluation was inappropriate. If the final decision holds that the evaluation performed is appropriate, the parent still has the right to an independent educational evaluation, but not at public expense.

3. Written notice must be provided to parents prior to a proposal or refusal to initiate or make a change in the child's identification, evaluation, or educational placement and must include the following:
   - A listing of parental due process safeguards
   - A description and a rationale for the chosen action
   - A detailed listing of the components (e.g., tests, records, reports) that were the basis for the decision
   - Assurance that the language and content of notices were understood by the parents

4. Parental consent must be obtained before evaluation procedures can occur unless parents or guardians cannot be identified to function in the due process role. When this occurs, a suitable person must be assigned to act as a surrogate. This is done by the LEA in full accordance with legislation.

Learn more about due process here: *http://www.wrightslaw.com/info/dp.index.htm*

COMPETENCY 008   UNDERSTAND HOW TO COMMUNICATE AND
                        COLLABORATE WITH OTHERS TO HELP STUDENTS
                        WITH DISABILITIES ACHIEVE DESIRED LEARNING
                        OUTCOMES

Skill 8.1   Demonstrating knowledge of family systems theory and the roles
                   of parents/guardians in the educational process (e.g., serving as
                   primary informal teachers of their children; collaborating in
                   designing, implementing, and evaluating IEPs, transition plans,
                   and behavioral plans)

The special educator should be knowledgeable of family systems, as well as the
impact of the systems on a family's response and contribution to the education of a
child with special needs. The family systems theory, as outlined on the Bowen
Center for the Study of the Family
(http://www.thebowencenter.org/pages/theory.html), has been developed by Murray
Bowen over recent decades. The Bowen Theory of Family Systems is outlined as
follows.

Triangles refer to the impact on existing relationships between two people in a family
when a third individual joins the family.

In the case of a child with a disability, it could refer to the impact of the child's needs
and associated physical, emotional, and financial stress on the marriage of the
parents.

Differentiation of self refers to the influence of family members to think alike and the
individual's ability to think critically and independently while realizing the realistic
extent of his or her need for others.

For example, in a family with a deaf child, the parents may be pressured by
grandparents not to have the child undergo a cochlear implant, due to the invasive
nature of the surgery. While the child's parents realize the importance of family
support and relationships, parents with a strong differentiation of self will consider all
the information and then make a decision that may go against the thoughts of the
grandparents.

Nuclear family emotional system describes four basic relationship patterns that can
develop or worsen because of tension. The patterns are *marital conflict, dysfunction
in one spouse, impairment of one or more children,* and *emotional distance.*

Because of the tension that results from the birth and parenting of a child with a
disability, any or all of the relationship patterns may develop.

Family projection process refers to the parental projection of a perception (such as
low self-esteem) or problem (learning disability) that results in the treatment of the

child as such. With time, the projection may become a self-fulfilling prophecy. The projection process follows three steps:

1. The parent focuses on a child out of fear that something is wrong with him or her
2. The parent interprets the child's behavior as confirming the fear
3. The parent treats the child as if something is really wrong

Multigenerational transmission process refers to the impact of parenting and the resulting differentiation of self on future generations.

In the case of the parents of a child with a disability, parents who have developed a stronger differentiation of self are more likely to acknowledge their child's disability (regardless of extended family perception of the social stigma it may bring) and to consider all options of treatment and educational programming for their child.

Emotional cutoff occurs when the individual distances him or herself from the family as an adult due to unresolved conflict.

In the case of a child with a disability, a parent may distance him or herself from his or her own parents because of their ongoing opinion that severely disabled children should be institutionalized. By the emotional cutoff between the child's parent and grandparents, ongoing emotional and physical support may be jeopardized or lost completely.

Sibling position is described in Bowen's work and is referenced as "incorporating the work of Walter Toman." According to sibling position, birth order reflects tendencies of children in later interactions. Firstborn children tend to be leaders; younger siblings tend to be followers.

Societal emotional process refers to the carryover of the above systems into all areas of personal interaction in the society (including the workplace and school). Hypothetical examples of how family systems affect special education students and their families are given above. The special educator should be aware of these systems as he or she interacts with families on a regular basis and communicates with them regarding IEP planning and considerations.

Skill 8.2   Demonstrating knowledge of how to assist parents/guardians in identifying resources in relation to their children's development and education

EFFECTIVE COMMUNICATION BETWEEN TEACHERS AND FAMILIES

Research proves that the more families are involved in a child's educational experience, the more that child will succeed academically. Families know students better than almost anyone and are a valuable resource for teachers of exceptional students. Often, an insight or observation from a family member or his or her reinforcement of school standards or activities means the difference between success and frustration in a teacher's work with children. Suggestions for relationship building and collaboration with parents and families include the following:

- Use laypersons' terms when communicating with families and make the communication available in the language of the home.
- Search out and engage family members' knowledge and skills in providing educational and therapeutic services to the student.
- Explore and discuss the concerns of families and help them find tactics for addressing those concerns.
- Plan collaborative meetings with children and their families and help them become active contributors to their educational team.
- Ensure that communications with and about families are confidential and conducted with respect for their privacy.
- Offer parents accurate and professionally presented information about the pedagogical and therapeutic work being done with their child. It is sometimes necessary to provide professional guidance about the child's disability or the techniques that will help. For example, the parent of a third grade child who reads at the first grade level checks out library books at the third grade level and insists that the child labor through trying to read them in the hope this will improve the child's reading skills. The teacher needs to explain that while it would be helpful for the parent to read that third grade level book *to* the child, books chosen for the *child* to read should be easy enough for the child to read about 95% of the text independently, even if this is below grade level. The teacher might help the parent find material that is age appropriate but written at the child's level.
- Keep parents abreast of their rights, of the kinds of practices that might violate them, and of available recourse if needed.
- Acknowledge and respect cultural differences.

One common difficulty occurs when teachers assume that involvement in education simply means that the parents show up to help at school events or participate in parental activities on campus. With this belief, many teachers devise clever strategies to increase parental involvement at school. However, just because a parent shows up to school and assists with an activity does not mean that the child will learn more. Many parents work all day long and cannot assist in the school. Teachers, therefore, have to think of different ways to encourage parental and family involvement in the educational process.

PARENT CONFERENCES

The parent-teacher conference is generally for one of three purposes. First, the teacher may wish to share information with the parents concerning the performance and behavior of the child. Second, the teacher may be interested in obtaining information from the parents about the child. Such information may help answer questions or concerns that the teacher has. A third purpose may be to request parent support or involvement in specific activities or requirements. In many situations, more than one of the purposes may be involved.

Planning the Conference

When a conference is scheduled, whether at the request of the teacher or parent, the teacher should allow sufficient time to prepare thoroughly. Collect all relevant information, samples of student work, records of behavior, and other items needed to help the parent understand the circumstances. It is also a good idea to compile a list of questions or concerns you wish to address. Arrange the time and location of the conference to provide privacy and to avoid interruptions.

Conducting the Conference

Begin the conference by putting the parents at ease. Take the time to establish a comfortable mood, but do not waste time with unnecessary small talk. Begin your discussion with positive comments about the student. Identify strengths and desirable attributes, but do not exaggerate.

As you address issues or areas of concern, be sure to focus on observable behaviors and concrete results or information. Do not make judgmental statements about parent or child. Share specific work samples, anecdotal records of behavior, etc., which demonstrate clearly the concerns you have. Be a good listener and hear the parents' comments and explanations. Such background information can be invaluable in understanding the needs and motivations of the child.

Finally, end the conference with an plan of action agreed between parents and teacher (and, when appropriate, the child). Bring the conference to a close politely but firmly and thank the parents for their involvement.

After the Conference

A day or two after the conference, it is a good idea to send a follow-up note to the parents. In this note, briefly and concisely reiterate the plan or step agreed to in the conference. Be polite and professional; avoid the temptation to be too informal or chatty. If the issue is a long term one such as the behavior or on-going work performance of the student, make periodic follow-up contacts to keep the parents informed of the progress.

Skill 8.3   **Applying knowledge of effective strategies for communicating, collaborating, and consulting with general education teachers, related services providers, other school staff members, medical professionals, and representatives of community agencies to provide services for students with disabilities and their families (e.g., providing learning opportunities, adapting and modifying curriculum and instruction, addressing mental health needs, engaging in transition planning)**

INSTRUCTIONAL PLANNING FOR A VARIETY OF INCLUSIVE MODELS (E.G., CO-TEACHING, PUSH-IN, CONSULTANT TEACHING [CT])

According to IDEA 2004, students with disabilities are to participate in the general education program to the extent that it is beneficial for them. As students are included in a variety of general education activities and classes, the need for collaboration among teachers grows.

Co-teaching

One model for general education teachers and special education teachers to use for collaboration is co-teaching. *In this model, both teachers actively teach in the general education classroom.* Perhaps both teachers will conduct a small science experiment group at the same time, switching groups at some point in the lesson. Perhaps in social studies, one teacher will lecture while the other teacher writes notes on the board or points out information on a map.

In the co-teaching model, the general education teacher and special educator often switch roles back and forth within a class period, or they may do so at the end of a chapter or unit.

Push-in Teaching

In the push-in teaching model, the special educator teaches parallel material in the general education classroom. When the regular education teacher teaches word problems in math, for example, the special educator may work with some students on setting up the initial problems, followed by having them complete the computation. Another example would be in science; when the general education teacher asks review questions for a test, the special educator works with a student who has a review study sheet to find the answer from a group of choices.

In the push-in teaching model, it may appear that two versions of the same lesson are being taught or that two types of student responses/activities are being monitored on the same material. The push-in teaching model is considered one type of differentiated instruction in which two teachers are teaching simultaneously.

Consultant Teaching

In the consultant teaching model, the general education teacher conducts the class after planning with the special educator how to differentiate activities so that the needs of the student with a disability are met.

In a social studies classroom using the consultant teaching model, both teachers may discuss what the expectations will be for a student with a learning disability and fine motor difficulty when the class does reports on states. They may decide that doing a state report is appropriate for the student; however, he or she may use the computer to write the report so that he or she can utilize the spell check feature and so that the work is legible.

COOPERATIVE NATURE OF THE TRANSITION PLANNING PROCESS

Transition planning is mandated in IDEA 1997. The transition planning requirements ensure that planning is begun at age 14 (changed in 2004 to 16) and continued through high school. Transition planning and services focus on a coordinated set of student-centered activities designed to facilitate the student's progression from school to post-school activities. Transition planning should be flexible and focus on the developmental and educational requirements of the student at different grades and times.

Transition planning must focus on providing instruction and training in vocational programming when possible and where related services outside the school environment can be tied into making a student's transition successful. It is also possible that transition planning could provide job opportunities that may lead beyond the school years and to the ability to achieve what may be considered normal independence.

State departments offer continued support in college environments and training schools and help those with disabilities find jobs. Other community resources that can help with the transition to the "real world" environment and provide some continuity as the emerging adult leaves the protective school environment should be pointed out to the student and parent.

Transition planning is a student-centered event that necessitates a collaborative endeavor. Transition planning involves input from parents and educators, but team members share the responsibility of making the student's transition a smooth one.

The student must play a key role in transition planning. This means asking the student to identify preferences and interests. The student should also attend meetings on transition planning. The degree of success experienced by the student in postsecondary educational settings depends on the student's degree of motivation, independence, self-direction, self-advocacy, and academic abilities developed in high school. Student participation in transition activities should be implemented as early as possible, no later than age 16.

The primary function of parents during transition planning is to encourage and assist students in planning and achieving their educational goals. Parents also should encourage students to cultivate independent decision-making and self-advocacy skills.

The result of effective transition from a secondary to a postsecondary education program is a student with a learning disability who is confident, independent, self motivated, and striving to achieve career goals. This effective transition can be achieved if the team consisting of the student, parents, and professional personnel work as a group to create and implement effective transition plans.

Skill 8.4 **Demonstrating knowledge of effective strategies for supervising, monitoring, and evaluating the activities of paraprofessionals, aides, volunteers, and peer tutors**

PARAPROFESSIONALS AND GENERAL EDUCATION TEACHERS

Paraprofessionals and general education teachers are also important collaborators with teachers of exceptional students. Although they may have daily exposure to exceptional students, they may not have the theoretical or practical experience to assure their effective interaction with such students. They do bring valuable perspective and opportunities for breadth and variety in an exceptional child's educational experience. General education teachers also offer curriculum and subject matter expertise and a high level of professional support, while paraprofessionals may provide insights born of their particular familiarity with individual students. CEC suggests that teachers can best collaborate with general education teachers and paraprofessionals by:

- Offering information about the characteristics and needs of children with exceptional learning needs
- Discussing and brainstorming ways to integrate children with exceptionalities into various settings within the school community
- Modeling best practices and instructional techniques and accommodations and coaching others in their use
- Keeping communication about children with exceptional learning needs and their families confidential
- Consulting with these colleagues in the assessment of individuals with exceptional learning needs
- Engaging them in group problem-solving and in developing, executing, and assessing collaborative activities
- Offering support to paraprofessionals by observing their work with students and offering feedback and suggestions

RELATED SERVICE PROVIDERS AND ADMINISTRATORS

Related service providers and administrators offer specialized skills and abilities that are critical to the exceptional education teacher's ability to advocate for his or her student and meet a school's legal obligations to the student and his or her family. *Related service providers—such as speech, occupational and language therapists, psychologists, and physicians—offer expertise and resources unparalleled in meeting a child's developmental needs.* Administrators are often experts in the resources available at the school and local education agency levels, as well as the culture and politics of a school system, and can be powerful partners in meeting the needs of exceptional education teachers and students.

A teacher's most effective approach to collaborating with these professionals includes the following:

- Confirming mutual understanding of the accepted goals and objectives of the student with exceptional learning needs as documented in his or her IEP
- Soliciting input about ways to support related service goals in classroom settings
- Understanding the needs and motivations of each professional and acting in support whenever possible
- Facilitating respectful and beneficial relationships between families and professionals
- Regularly and accurately communicating observations and data about the child's progress or challenges

Working Together

This section will specifically address the working relationship teachers should have with their colleagues in the classroom environment. There are six basic steps to having a rewarding collaborative relationship, whether the others are paraprofessionals, aides, or volunteers.

While it is understood that there are many types of colleagues who may be assisting in a classroom, this section will summarize their titles as "classroom assistant."

1. **Get to know each other.**
   The best way to start a relationship with anyone is to find time alone to get to know each other. Give a new classroom assistant the utmost respect and look at this as an opportunity to share talents and learn those of a coworker. Remember that this is the opportunity to find places of agreement and disagreement, which can help maintain and build a working relationship. Good working relationships require the knowledge of where each other's strengths and weaknesses are. This knowledge may create one of one of the best working relationships possible.

2. **Remember that communication is a two-way street.**
   As a professional educator, it is important to remember that one must actively communicate with others. This is especially important with classroom assistants. Listen to them and let them know that listening is taking place. Pay attention and make sure that the classroom assistant sees an incorporation of his or her thoughts. Encourage them to engage conversations by asking for more information. Asking a classroom assistant for details and insights may help to further meet the needs of students. It is also an educator's responsibility to remove and prevent communication barriers in the working relationship. Avoid giving negative criticism or put downs. Do not "read" motivations into the actions of the classroom assistant. Learn about them through open communication.

3. **Establish clear roles and responsibilities.**
   The Access Center for Improving Outcomes of All Students K-8 has defined these roles in the table below.

	Teacher Role	**Classroom Assistant Role**	**Areas of Communication**
Instruction	• Plan all instruction, including expected goals/objectives in small groups • Provide instruction in whole-class settings	• Work with small groups of students on specific tasks, including review or re-teaching of content • Work with one student at a time to provide intensive instruction or remediation on a concept or skill	• Teachers provide specific content and guidance about curriculum, students and instructional materials • Classroom assistants note student progress and give feedback to teachers
Curriculum & Lesson Plan Development	• Develop all lesson plans and instructional materials • Ensure alignment with standards, student needs, and IEPs	• Provide assistance in development of classroom activities, retrieval of materials, and coordination of activities	• Mutual review of lesson plan components prior to class • Teachers provide guidance about specific instructional methods
Classroom Management	• Develop and guide class-wide management plans for behavior and classroom structures	• Assist with the implementation of class-wide and individual behavior management plans • Monitor hallways,	• Teachers provide guidance about specific behavior management strategies and student

	▪ Develop and monitor individual behavior management plans	study hall, and other activities outside normal class	characteristics ▪ Classroom assistants note student progress and activities and give feedback to teachers

"Working Together: Teacher-Paraeducator Collaboration," The Access Center for Improving Outcomes of All Students K-8, http://www.k8accesscenter.org/training_resources/documents/Tchr-ParaCollaboration.pdf

4. **Plan together.**
    Planning together lets the classroom assistant know they are considered valuable. It also provides a timeline of expectations that will aid in the overall classroom delivery to students. This also gives the impression to students that all authority figures are on the same page and know what is going to happen next.
5. **Show a united front.**
    It is essential to let students know that both adults in the room deserve the same amount of respect. Have a plan in place on how to address negative behaviors individually as well as together. *Do not* make a statement in front of the students that the classroom assistant is wrong. Take time to address issues regarding class time privately, not in front of the class.
6. **Reevaluate your relationship.**
    Feedback is wonderful. Stop every now and then and discuss how the team is working. Be willing to listen to suggestions. Taking this time may be the opportunity to improve the working relationship.

Additional Reading: "Creating a Classroom Team," http://www.aft.org/pubs-reports/psrp/classroom_team.pdf.

Skill 8.5   Applying knowledge of small-group processes and effective strategies for facilitating child study teams, IEP-planning teams, and transition-planning teams

REVIEW OF STUDENT NEEDS WITH INCLUSION TEACHER AND SUPPORT STAFF

It may be determined at a student's IEP meeting that some time in the general education setting is appropriate. The activities and classes listed for inclusion may be field trips, lunch, recess, physical education, music, library, art, computers, math, science, social studies, spelling, reading, and/or English. The IEP will specify which classes and activities, as well as the amount of time that the student will spend with general education peers. The IEP will also list any modifications or accommodations that will be needed.

Modifications that may be considered for the general education classroom include the amount of work or type of task required. Modifications for a student with a learning disability might include a reduced number of spelling words or a task of writing the vocabulary word that goes with a given definition instead of writing the definition that goes with a given word.

Accommodations are changes made to the school environment or a student's use of necessary equipment to overcome a disability. For example, an accommodation for a student with a hearing impairment might include the use of an auditory trainer or another student to serve as a notetaker.

Prior to the student starting in a general education placement (regardless of the minutes on the IEP), the general education teacher and support staff (if any) should be in-serviced on the student's disability and his or her needs according to the IEP. Sometimes this in-servicing happens as the student's IEP is developed. Other times it is done at a later date.

STUDENT EXPECTATIONS IN THE INCLUSION SETTING

The student with a disability should be well aware of his or her responsibilities in the general education setting ahead of time. These expectations should be a combination of behavior and task performance. Although students should be aware of needed accommodations and modifications, and should be self-advocates for such, they should not use their disabilities as excuses for not fulfilling the expectations.

Students may benefit from previewing material, using a checklist to keep track of materials and assignments, keeping an assignment notebook, reviewing materials after the lesson, and using study aids such as flashcards. Sometimes, a behavior tracking chart may also be used.

Monitoring Student Progress in the Inclusion Setting

Once the student is in the general education setting for the time and activities listed on the IEP, the special education teacher will need to monitor student progress. This can be done through verbal follow-up with the general education teacher or by asking the teacher to complete a progress form periodically. Of course, grades and the student's ability to restate learned information or answer questions are also indicators.

Evaluation of the Student's Future Placement in the Inclusion Setting

If the student is successful in the general education activities and classes listed on the IEP, the special education teacher may consider easing back on modifications and accommodations on the next IEP. He or she may also consider adding minutes or classes for student's general education inclusion.

If the student has difficulty in the general education activities and classes, the special educator may consider adding more modifications or accommodations on the next IEP. If the student had significant difficulty, he or she may need to receive more services in the special education classroom.

Also see to the Inclusion section of 7.1.

Sample Test

Directions: Select the best answer in each group.

UNDERSTANDING STUDENTS WITH DISABILITIES

1. Joey is in a mainstreamed preschool program. One of the means his teacher uses in determining growth in adaptive skills is that of observation. Some questions about Joey's behavior that she might ask include the following:
    (Average) (Skill 1.1)

    A. Is he able to hold a cup?

    B. Can he call the name of any of his toys?

    C. Can he reach for an object and grasp it?

    D. All of the above

2. Which of the following statements about children with emotional/behavioral disorders is true?
    (Average) (Skill 1.1)

    A. They have very high IQs.

    B. They display poor social skills.

    C. They are poor academic achievers.

    D. Both B and C

3. Which behavior would be expected at the mild level of emotional/behavioral disorders?
    (Rigorous) (Skill 1.1)

    A. Attention seeking

    B. Inappropriate affect

    C. Self-injurious actions

    D. Poor sense of identity

4. Which category of behaviors would most likely be found on a behavior rating scale?
    (Easy) (Skill 1.1)

    A. Disruptive, acting out

    B. Shy, withdrawn

    C. Aggressive (physical or verbal)

    D. All of the above

5. **The social skills of students in mental retardation programs are likely to be appropriate for children of their mental age rather than chronological age. This means that the teacher will need to do all of the following except:**
    (Easy) (Skill 1.1)

    A. Model desired behavior

    B. Provide clear instructions

    C. Expect age appropriate behaviors

    D. Adjust the physical environment when necessary

6. **Which of the following examples would be considered of highest priority when determining the need for the delivery of appropriate special education and related services?**
    (Rigorous) (Skill 1.1)

    A. An eight-year-old boy is repeating first grade for the second time and exhibits problems with toileting, gross motor functions, and remembering number and letter symbols. His regular classroom teacher claims the referral forms are too time-consuming and refuses to complete them. The teacher also refuses to make accommodations because he feels every child should be treated alike.

    B. A six-year-old girl who has been diagnosed as autistic is placed in a special education class within the local school. Her mother wants her to attend residential school next year, even though the girl is showing progress.

    C. A ten-year-old girl with profound mental retardation is receiving education services in a state institution.

    D. A twelve-year-old boy with mild disabilities is placed in a behavior disorders program but displays obvious perceptual deficits (e.g., reversal of letters and symbols, an inability to discriminate sounds). He was originally thought to have a learning disability but did not meet state criteria for this exceptionality category based on results of standard scores. He has always had problems with attending to tasks and is now beginning to get into trouble during seatwork time. His teacher feels that he will eventually become a real behavior problem. He receives social skills training in the resource room one period a day.

7. **The Carrow Elicited Language Inventory is a test designed to give the examiner diagnostic information about a child's expressive grammatical competence. Which of the following language components is being assessed?**
(Rigorous) (Skill 1.1)

   A.   Phonology

   B.   Morphology

   C.   Syntax

   D.   Both B and C

8. **In a Test of Psycholinguistic Abilities, the child is presented with a picture representing statements, such as the following: "Here is one die; here are two ____." This test is essentially a test of:**
(Rigorous) (Skill 1.1)

   A.   Phonology

   B.   Morphology

   C.   Syntax

   D.   Semantics

9. **Five-year-old Tom continues to substitute the "w" sound for the "r" sound when pronouncing words; therefore, he often distorts words (e.g., "wabbit" for "rabbit" and "wat" for "rat"). His articulation disorder is basically a problem in:**
(Rigorous) (Skill 1.1)

   A.   Phonology

   B.   Morphology

   C.   Syntax

   D.   Semantics

10. **Which of the following is untrue about the ending "er?"**
(Rigorous) (Skill 1.1)

   A.   It is an example of a free morpheme.

   B.   It represents one of the smallest units of meaning within a word.

   C.   It is called an inflectional ending.

   D.   When added to a word, it connotes a comparative status

11. **Which component of language involves language content rather than the form of language?**
(Rigorous) (Skill 1.1)

A. Phonology

B. Morphology

C. Semantics

D. Syntax

12. **Which is least indicative of a developmental delay?**
(Rigorous) (Skill 1.1)

A. Language and speech production

B. Gross motor skills

C. Self-help skills

D. Arithmetic computation skills

13. **A child with intellectual disabilities who is fairly clumsy and possesses poor social awareness—but who can be taught to communicate and to perform semiskilled labor and maintains himself under supervision—probably belongs to which level of classification as an adult?**
(Rigorous) (Skill 1.1)

A. Mild

B. Moderate

C. Severe

D. Profound

14. **All of the following are common characteristics of a student who is emotionally disturbed *except*:**
(Average) (Skill 1.1)

A. Socially accepted by peers

B. Highly disruptive to the classroom environment

C. Academic difficulties

D. Areas of talent overlooked by a teacher

15. **Duration is an appropriate measure to take with all of these behaviors EXCEPT:**
(Easy) (Skill 1.2)

   A.   Thumb sucking

   B.   Hitting

   C.   Temper tantrums

   D.   Maintaining eye contact

16. **All children cry, hit, fight, and play alone, at different times. Children with behavior disorders will perform these behaviors at a higher than normal:**
(Average) (Skill 1.2)

   A.   Rate

   B.   Topography

   C.   Duration

   D.   Magnitude

17. **Which of the following is typical of attention problems that a youngster with a learning disability might display?**
(Rigorous) (Skill 1.2)

   A.   Lack of selective attention

   B.   Does not consider consequences before acting

   C.   Unable to Control Own Actions or impulses

   D.   Poor fine motor coordination

18. **Echolalia, repetitive stereotyped actions, and a severe disorder of thinking and communication are indicative of:**
(Rigorous) (Skill 1.2)

   A.   Psychosis

   B.   Schizophrenia

   C.   Autism

   D.   Paranoia

19. **In which of the following exceptionality categories may a student be considered for inclusion if his IQ score falls more than two standard deviations below the mean?**
(Rigorous) (Skill 1.2)

    A.   Mental Retardation

    B.   Specific Learning Disabilities

    C.   Emotionally/Behaviorally Disordered

    D.   Gifted

20. **Individuals with mild mental retardation can be characterized as:**
(Rigorous) (Skill 1.2)

    A.   Often indistinguishable from normal developing children at an early age

    B.   Having a higher than normal rate of motor activity

    C.   Displaying significant discrepancies in ability levels

    D.   Uneducable in academic skills

21. **Which characteristic is *not* often present in children with profound multidisabilities?**
(Easy) (Skill 1.3)

    A.   Self-stimulation (rocking, hand-flapping)

    B.   Frequently nonambulatory

    C.   Excessively social and responsive to others

    D.   Aggressiveness toward others

22. **Why must teachers maintain a positive attitude, and avoid bias?**
(Average) (Skill 2.4)

    A.   Positive attitudes enable a student to potentially believe in his or her abilities more.

    B.   Cultures and religions have different views.

    C.   Teaching is a calling; not a job.

    D.   Positivity provides optimism.

23. **What type of medication is often used to treat depression and obsessive-compulsive behavior?**
(Average) (Skill 2.5)

   A.   Oxidase inhibitors

   B.   Tricyclic antidepressants.

   C.   Selective serotonin-reuptake inhibitors

   D.   Stimulants

24. **Why must educators be aware of medication students may be taking?**
(Rigorous) (Skill 2.5)

   A.   Medications can complicate curricular plans.

   B.   Many medications cause side effects.

   C.   Teachers can be more sensitive to the students' behaviors and attention spans.

   D.   All of the above

ASSESSING STUDENTS AND DEVELOPING PROGRAMS

25. **Which of the following is NOT an appropriate assessment modification or accommodation for a student with a learning disability?**
(Average) (Skill 3.1)

   A.   Having the test read orally to the student

   B.   Writing down the student's dictated answers

   C.   Allowing the student to take the assessment home to complete

   D.   Extending the time for the student to take the assessment

26. **Children who write poorly might be given tests that allow oral responses unless the purpose for the test is to:**
(Average) (Skill 3.1)

   A.   Assess handwriting skills

   B.   Test for organization of thoughts

   C.   Answer questions pertaining to math reasoning

   D.   Assess rote memory

27. **The purpose of error analysis of a test is to:**
(Easy) (Skill 3.1)

   A. Determine what events were labeled in error

   B. Determine if the test length was the cause of error

   C. Evaluate the types of errors made by categorizing incorrect answers

   D. Establish a baseline

28. **You are working with a functional program and have placed a student in a vocational position in the kitchen of a coffee house. A waiter takes orders and relays them to the student, whose job is to make the coffee as ordered. You need to perform a task analysis of making a cup of coffee. Which task should be first in the analysis?**
(Average) (Skill 3.1)

   A. Filling the pot with water

   B. Taking the order

   C. Measuring the coffee

   D. Picking the correct coffee

29. **How are informal assessments quantified and measured?**
(Average) (Skill 3.1)

   A. Via observational notes

   B. They cannot be quantified

   C. Decile scoring

   D. Percentile ranking

30. **Standardized tests allow:**
(Easy) (Skill 3.1)

   A. Administration to groups

   B. Administration to individuals

   C. Comparison across population

   D. All of the above

31. **What are individual intelligence tests used for primarily?**
(Average) (Skill 3.1)

   A. Program placement in a classroom

   B. Classification

   C. Defining a person's potential

   D. Screening groups

32. **Formal assessments include standardized tests, norm-referenced Instruments, and:**
(Rigorous) (Skill 3.1)

   A. Developmental rating scales

   B. Interviews

   C. Anecdotes/ Observations

   D. Textbook chapter tests

33. **Which of the following is an advantage of giving informal individual assessments, rather than standardized group tests?**
(Easy) (Skill 3.1)

   A. Questions can be modified to reveal a specific student's strategies or misconceptions.

   B. The test administrator can clarify or rephrase questions for the student.

   C. They can be inserted into the class quickly on an as needed basis.

   D. All of the above

34. **Criterion referenced tests can provide information about:**
(Rigorous) (Skill 3.1)

   A. Whether a student has mastered prerequisite skills

   B. Whether a student is ready to proceed to the next level of instruction

   C. Which instructional materials might be helpful in covering program objectives

   D. All of the above

35. **The extent to which a test measures what it claims to measure is called:**
(Rigorous) (Skill 3.2)

   A. Reliability

   B. Validity

   C. Factor analysis

   D. Chi Square

36. **Acculturation refers to the individual's:**
(Rigorous) (Skill 3.3)

   A. Gender

   B. Experiential background

   C. Social class

   D. Ethnic background

37. **What type of data does a teacher organize and prepare for student evaluations?**
(Average) (Skill 4.1)

   A. Reason for assessment

   B. Test results

   C. Educational recommendations

   D. All of the above

38. **What is the purpose of teacher assistance teams?**
(Average) (Skill 4.2)

   A. Make professional suggestions

   B. Recommend instructional modifications

   C. Offer curricular alternatives

   D. All of the above

39. **Why provide a student with a checklist or check sheet?**
(Average) (Skill 4.2)

   A. Students cannot track their accomplishments.

   B. Check sheets are markers of success.

   C. Checklists provide loose structure.

   D. Check sheets relate material that is relevant to the student.

40. **Why should teachers use a variety of assessment techniques?**
(Easy) (Skill 4.3)

   A. To understand the benefits of assessments

   B. To determine the existing knowledge, skills, needs

   C. To offer numerical data to state regulatory agencies

   D. All of the above

41. **What is the purpose of diagnosis via assessment?**
(Average) (Skill 4.3)

   A. To identify students who are not ready for new material

   B. To scan the classroom for additional data

   C. To find students who can answer all questions

   D. To understand the classroom as a whole

42. **What is the ultimate goal of diagnostic endeavors?**
(Average) (Skill 4.3)

A. Find students who do well

B. Create tests

C. Gather data on certain topics

D. Improve learning

43. **How should assessment information be used?**
(Average) (Skill 4.3)

A. To provide performance-based criteria

B. To set academic expectations

C. To identify areas of weakness

D. All of the above

44. **Why is it important that teachers make inferences?**
(Rigorous) (Skill 4.3)

A. Teachers can verify factual data.

B. They can guess why a student is struggling.

C. They can gather definitive information about projected student performance.

D. They can learn about the students.

45. **How should intelligence test scores be interpreted?**
(Rigorous) (Skill 4.3)

A. In terms of the person's potential

B. In terms of the class potential

C. In terms of performance

D. In terms of test reliability

46. **Which terms should a teacher become familiar with when conducting and interpreting tests?**
(Average) (Skill 4.3)

A. Standardized information

B. Relativity to the student population

C. Interpretation of charts and graphs

D. All of the above

47. **Which of the following purposes of testing calls for an informal test?**
(Rigorous) (Skill 4.3)

   A. Screening a group of children to determine their readiness for the first reader

   B. Analyzing the responses of a student with a disability to various presentations of content material to see which strategy works for him

   C. Evaluating the effectiveness of a fourth-grade math program at the end of its first year of use in a specific school

   D. Determining the general level of intellectual functioning of a class of fifth graders

48. **A transition or vocational curriculum approach focuses on:**
(Rigorous) (Skill 4.4)

   A. Remediation of basic academic skills

   B. Preparation for functioning in society as adults

   C. Preparation for the world of work

   D. Daily living and social skills

49. **Which of the following is an important principle when a student is transitioning from one program or setting to another?**
(Average) (Skill 4.4)

   A. Services should be interrupted temporarily until new services are available in the new setting.

   B. Transition should include duplication in assessment and goal planning.

   C. All student records should be transferred to the new setting so that no ongoing communication is necessary.

   D. Transition should be viewed as a process.

50. **Transition planning should involve all of the following except**
(Easy) (Skill 4.4)

   A. Service coordinators

   B. Families

   C. Other students

   D. Teachers

51. **What is the purpose of keeping student portfolios?**
(Average) (Skill 4.5)

   A. Compile student work

   B. Monitor progress over a period of time

   C. Presentation for parent-teacher conference

   D. All of the above

PROMOTING STUDENT DEVELOPMENT AND LEARNING

52. **What is one way to differentiate the class in a large group setting?**
Average) (Skill 5.1)

   A. Modify instruction time

   B. Avoid visual aids

   C. Do not allow breaks

   D. Establish a rule

53. **Who determines peer tutoring goals?**
(Average) (Skill 5.1)

   A. Peers

   B. IEP team

   C. Teachers

   D. Consultant teachers

54. **Which type of grouping arrangement would be MOST effective for teaching basic academic skills such as math facts or reading?**
(Rigorous) (Skill 5.1)

   A. Large group with teacher

   B. Peer tutoring

   C. Small group instruction

   D. Cooperative learning

55. **How is student motivation increased when classroom instruction is modified?**
(Average) (Skill 5.2)

   A. Students can manipulate materials that they use in their lives.

   B. Students can practice new skills.

   C. Students can process material easier.

   D. Information is relevant to the student.

56. **Teaching techniques that stimulate active participation and understanding in the mathematics class include all but which of the following?** *(Easy) (Skill 5.2)*

   A. Having students copy computation facts for a set number of times.

   B. Asking students to find the error in an algorithm.

   C. Giving immediate feedback to students.

   D. Having students chart their progress.

57. **The social skills of students with mental retardation disabilities are likely to be appropriate for children of their mental age, rather than chronological age. This means that the teacher whose class contains children with these disabilities will need to do all of the following except:** *(Easy) (Skill 5.2)*

   A. Model desired behavior

   B. Provide clear instructions

   C. Expect age appropriate behaviors

   D. Adjust the physical environment when necessary

58. **Modifications in the classroom include which of the following:** *(Average) (Skill 5.2)*

   A. Reduced number of spelling words on the weekly quiz

   B. Highlighting and clarifying directions

   C. Providing a word bank

   D. All of the above

59. **All of the following are suggestions for *pacing* or altering the presentation of tasks to match the student's rate of learning except:** *(Average) (Skill 5.3)*

   A. Teach in several shorter segments of time rather than a single lengthy session

   B. Continue to teach a task until the lesson is completed in order to provide more time on task

   C. Watch for nonverbal cues that indicate students are becoming confused, bored, or restless

   D. Avoid giving students an inappropriate amount of written work

60. The rule is "no talking during silent reading time." Mrs. Jenkins gives her students 20 minutes each Friday to quietly read a book or magazine of their choice. And every Friday, Karl turns to talk to Jake. What non-aversive technique may Mrs. Jenkins employ to reduce this undesirable behavior?
(Rigorous) (Skill 5.3)

A. Self-assessment

B. Planned ignoring

C. Proximity control

D. Token economy

61. How can a teacher decide when rules are broken or complied with?
(Average) (Skill 5.3)

A. A system of positive consequences, or rewards, can promote a positive classroom.

B. Positive expectations give the teacher an assertive response style

C. Setting limits allows students to refrain from negative behavior.

D. All of the above.

62. When developing a management plan, teachers must be:
(Average) (Skill 5.3)

A. Focused on reward systems

B. Open to students dictating the rules

C. Proactive

D. Sole developer of rationale

63. In establishing a classroom behavior management plan with the students, it is best to:
(Average) (Skill 5.3)

A. Have rules written and in place on day one

B. Hand out a copy of the rules to the students on day one

C. Have separate rules for each class on day one

D. Have students involved in creating the rules on day one

64. **Laura is beginning to raise her hand first instead of talking out. An effective schedule of reinforcement should be:**
(Average) (Skill 5.3)

A. Continuous

B. Variable

C. Intermittent

D. Fixed

65. **Which of the following is NOT a feature of effective classroom rules?**
(Easy) (Skill 5.3)

A. They are about four to six in number

B. They are negatively stated

C. Consequences are consistent and immediate

D. They can be tailored to individual teaching goals and teaching styles

66. **What is *not* an example of the use of a punishment procedure?**
(Rigorous) (Skill 5.3)

A. Ted quit talking with Jim when Mrs. Green frowned at him.

B. Timmy stopped getting out of his seat when the teacher scolded him.

C. Mary completed her math when her teacher told her she would have to miss recess if she wasn't through with the work.

D. Fred stopped making funny faces when Mrs. Smith placed him in time out.

67. **Mr. Smith is on a field trip with a group of high school EH students. On the way, they stop at a fast-food restaurant for lunch, and Warren and Raul get into an argument. After some heated words, Warren stalks out of the restaurant and refuses to return to the group. He leaves the parking lot, continues walking away from the group, and ignores Mr. Smith's directions to come back. What would be the best course of action for Mr. Smith?**
(Rigorous) (Skill 5.4)

A. Leave the group with the class aide and follow Warren to try to talk him into coming back

B. Wait a little while and see if Warren cools off and returns

C. Telephone the school and let the crisis teacher notify the police in accordance with school policy

D. Call the police himself

68. **What are organizers?**
(Easy) (Skill 6.1)

A. Learning tools

B. Visual aids

C. Diagrams

D. All of the above

69. **To facilitate learning instructional objectives:**
(Average) (Skill 6.1)

A. They should be taken from a grade-level spelling list

B. They should be written and shared

C. They should be arranged in order of similarity

D. They should be taken from a scope and sequence

70. **Which of the following is a good example of a generalization?**
(Average) (Skill 6.1)

A. Jim has learned to add and is now ready to subtract

B. Sarah adds sets of units to obtain a product

C. Bill recognizes a vocabulary word on a billboard when traveling

D. Jane can spell the word "net" backwards to get the word "ten"

71. **John learns best through the auditory channel, so his teacher wants to reinforce his listening skills. Through which of the following types of equipment would instruction be most effectively presented?**
(Easy) (Skill 6.2)

A. Overhead Projector

B. CD Player

C. Microcomputer

D. Opaque Projector

72. **What Assistive Technology (AT) is best for Bob, who can compose well, but has difficulty with both encoding and the physical act of writing?**
(Average) (Skill 6.2)

A. A peer to write what he dictates

B. Voice to text computer software

C. A CD player he can listen to while others write

D. A slant board for writing

73. **When a student begins to use assistive technology, it is important for the teacher to have a clear outline as to when and how the equipment should be used. Why?**
(Rigorous) (Skill 6.2)

A. To establish a level of accountability with the student.

B. To establish that the teacher has responsibility for the equipment that is in use in his or her room.

C. To establish that the teacher is responsible for the usage of the assistive technology.

D. To establish a guideline for evaluation.

74. **What criteria must be considered when choosing assistive technology (AT) to help a particular student?** *(Easy) (Skill 6.2)*

    A. Whether there is a specific need the AT can meet (e.g., a goal on the IEP that requires it)

    B. The degree of independence with which the student can use the device

    C. The need for collaborative planning for the device to be used across all relevant settings and transfer between settings

    D. All of the above

75. **There are several types of AT devices. They include:** *(Rigorous) (Skill 6.2)*

    A. Graphic Organizers

    B. Hearing Aides

    C. Handwritten Notes

    D. Supply Cases

76. **Learning tools are offered in both low-tech and high-tech options. What can be used for math class?** *(Average) (Skill 6.2)*

    A. Notebook paper

    B. Manipulatives

    C. Text books

    D. Lab tables

WORKING IN A PROFESSIONAL ENVIRONMENT

77. **What made the Smith v. Robinson (1984) case significant?** *(Rigorous) (Skill 7.1)*

    A. Attorney's fees would be paid to parents who won litigation.

    B. Students could not be denied an education due to behavior

    C. Specific health services became mandated

    D. "Free and Public" Education was established.

78. One of the most important goals of the special education teacher is to foster and create with the student:
(Easy) (Skill 7.1)

   A.   Handwriting skills

   B.   Self-advocacy

   C   An increased level of reading

   D.   Logical reasoning

79. Greg is a three-year-old boy who has recently survived a bout of meningitis. The pediatrician who treated Greg during his illness had to inform Greg's parents about some brain dysfunction which he had medically diagnosed. A reaction which would be anticipated upon learning of Greg's condition is:
(Easy) (Skill 7.1)

   A.   Shock

   B.   Disbelief

   C.   Denial

   D.   All of the Above

80. Early 19th century is considered a period of great importance in the field of special education because principles presently used in working with exceptional students were formulated by Itard. These principles included:
(Average) (Skill 7.1)

   A.   Individualized instruction

   B.   Sequence of tasks

   C.   Functional life-like skills curriculum

   D.   All of the above

81. Acceptance of disabilities by parents and siblings is most influenced by:
(Rigorous) (Skill 7.1)

   A.   Students obtain career training from elementary through high school

   B.   Students acquire specific training in job skills prior to exiting school

   C.   Students need specific training and supervision in applying skills learned in school to requirements in job situations

   D.   Students obtain needed instruction and field-based experiences that help them to be able to work in specific occupations

82. **Students with disabilities develop greater self-images and recognize their own academic and social strengths when they are:**
(Easy) (Skill 7.1)

   A. Included in the mainstream classroom

   B. Provided community based internships

   C. Socializing in the hallway

   D. Provided 1:1 instructional opportunity

83. **Society has normalized views toward those who are physically disabled by:**
(Easy) (Skill 7.1)

   A. Providing normal living arrangements

   B. Offering access to public facilities

   C. Making improvements in the media

   D. All of the above

84. **Which of the following must be completed before comprehensive testing occurs?**
(Average) (Skill 7.2)

   A. Teacher consult on student needs

   B. Pre-CSE conference

   C. Parental permission for each test

   D. All of the above

85. **What does Zero Reject require for all children with disabilities?**
(Rigorous) (Skill 7.2)

   A. Full inclusion of ALL students with disabilities in regular education classrooms and reporting annually

   B. Seeking out and providing services to ALL students with disabilities regardless of type or severity and reporting annually

   C. Free, appropriate public education provided to ALL students

   D. Both B and C

86. **How can a school violate the IDEA law?**
(Average) (Skill 7.2)

A. The school fails to adequately search for students with disabilities.

B. The school takes too long identifying and providing services to a child.

C. The school fails to provide services listed in the IEP.

D. All of the above

87. **How can a teacher violate the IDEA law?**
(Rigorous) (Skill 7.2)

A. A teacher does not provide modifications required by the IEP.

B. A teacher teaches in one style and does not differentiate.

C. A teacher does not utilize and work in conjunction with the paraprofessional staff accordingly.

D. A teacher does not utilize the technology in the room, i.e. Smartboard.

88. **According to IDEA 2004, students with disabilities are to do what?**
(Rigorous) (Skill 7.2)

A. Participate in the general education program to the fullest extent that it is beneficial for them

B. Participate in a vocational training program within the general education setting

C. Participate in a general education program for physical education

D. Participate in a Full Inclusion program that meets their needs

89. **Jacob's mother describes him as her "little leader." He organizes games at home, takes responsibility for setting the table, and initiates play. She states that her other, younger son is more of a follower; he is aloof and does not seem to stand up for himself. This demonstrates:**
(Average) (Skill 8.1)

A. Triangles

B. Sibling Position

C. Nuclear Family Emotional System

D. Family Projection Process

90. **All of the following are essential components of effective parent-teacher conferences EXCEPT:**
(Easy) (Skill 8.2)

A. Collecting samples of student work, records of behavior, and other relevant information

B. Beginning the conference with positive comments about the student

C. Using informal small talk to put the parents at ease

D. Preparing a list of questions or concerns you wish to address

91. **Parent contact should first begin when:**
(Average) (Skill 8.2)

A. You are informed the child will be your student.

B. The student fails a test.

C. The student exceeds others on a task.

D. An IEP meeting is scheduled and you have had no previous replies to letters.

92. **What can you do to create a good working environment with a classroom assistant?**
(Rigorous) (Skill 8.3)

A. Plan lessons with the assistant.

B. Write a contract that clearly defines his/her responsibilities in the classroom.

C. Remove previously given responsibilities.

D. All of the above

93. **Which of the following describes the push-in teaching model?**
(Easy) (Skill 8.3)

A. The general education teacher conducts the class while the special educator assists a student with disabilities one-on-one.

B. The special educator teaches parallel material in the general education classroom.

C. Both teachers actively teach in the general education classroom.

D. The general education teacher conducts the class after planning with the special educator how to differentiate activities to meet the needs of students with disabilities.

94. **Janice requires occupational therapy and speech therapy services. She is your student. What must you do to ensure her needs are met?** *(Rigorous) (Skill 8.4)*

    A.   Watch the services being rendered.

    B.   Schedule collaboratively.

    C.   Ask for services to be given in a push-in model.

    D.   Ask them to train you to give the service.

95. **What can a teacher do to create a good working environment with a classroom assistant?** *(Rigorous) (Skill 8.4)*

    A.   Plan lessons with the assistant.

    B.   Write a contract that clearly defines his or her responsibilities in the classroom.

    C.   Remove previously given responsibilities.

    D.   All of the above

96. **Which is a less-than-ideal example of collaboration in successful inclusion?** *(Rigorous) (Skill 8.4)*

    A.   Special education teachers are part of the instructional team in a regular classroom

    B.   Special education teachers are informed of the lesson beforehand and assist regular education teachers in the classroom

    C.   Teaming approaches are used for problem solving and program Implementation

    D.   Regular teachers, special education teachers, and other specialists or support teachers co-teach

97. **A paraprofessional has been assigned to assist you in the classroom. What action on the part of the teacher would lead to a poor working relationship?**
(Average) (Skill 8.4)

A. Having the paraprofessional lead a small group

B. Telling the paraprofessional what you expect him/her to do

C. Defining classroom behavior management as your responsibility alone

D. Taking an active role in his/her evaluation

98. **Mrs. Freud is a consultant teacher. She has two students with Mr. Ricardo. Mrs. Freud should:**
(Rigorous) (Skill 8.4)

A. Co-teach

B. Spend two days a week in the classroom helping out

C. Discuss lessons with the teacher and suggest modifications before class

D. Pull her students out for instructional modifications

99. **The most important member of the transition team is the**
(Easy) (Skill 8.5)

A. Parent

B. Student

C. Secondary personnel

D. Postsecondary personnel

100. **If it is determined at a student's IEP meeting that some time in the general education setting is appropriate, which activities and/or classes *might* be included?**
(Easy) (Skill 8.5)

A. Physical education

B. Math

C. Field trips

D. All of the above

Answer Key

1. D	35. B	69. C
2. D	36. B	70. C
3. A	37. D	71. B
4. D	38. D	72. B
5. C	39. B	73. A
6. A	40. B	74. D
7. C	41. A	75. B
8. C	42. D	76. B
9. A	43. D	77. A
10. A	44. C	78. B
11. C	45. C	79. D
12. D	46. D	80. D
13. B	47. B	81. C
14. A	48. B	82. A
15. B	49. D	83. D
16. A	50. C	84. C
17. A	51. D	85. D
18. C	52. A	86. D
19. A	53. C	87. A
20. A	54. C	88. A
21. C	55. A	89. B
22. A	56. A	90. C
23. B	57. C	91. A
24. D	58. D	92. A
25. C	59. B	93. B
26. A	60. C	94. B
27. C	61. D	95. A
28. D	62. C	96. B
29. A	63. D	97. C
30. D	64. A	98. C
31. B	65. B	99. B
32. D	66. C	100. D
33. D	67. C	
34. A	68. D	

Rigor Table

Question	Easy 20%	Average Rigor 40%	Rigorous 40%
	4, 5, 15, 21, 27, 30, 33, 40, 50, 56, 57, 65, 68, 71, 74, 78, 79, 82, 83, 90, 93, 99, 100	1, 2, 14, 16, 22, 23, 25, 26, 28, 29, 31, 37, 38, 39, 41, 42, 43, 46, 49, 51, 52, 53, 55, 58, 59, 61, 62, 63, 64, 69, 70, 72, 76, 80, 84, 86, 89, 91, 97	3, 6, 7, 8, 9, 10, 11, 12, 13, 17, 18, 19, 20, 24, 32, 34, 35, 36, 44, 45, 47, 48, 54, 60, 66, 67, 73, 75, 77, 81, 85, 87, 88, 92, 94, 95, 96, 98

Rationales with Sample Questions

Directions: Select the best answer in each group.

UNDERSTANDING STUDENTS WITH DISABILITIES

1.   Joey is in a mainstreamed preschool program. One of the means his teacher uses in determining growth in adaptive skills is that of observation. Some questions about Joey's behavior that she might ask include the following:
      (Average) (Skill 1.1)

      A.   Is he able to hold a cup?

      B.   Can he call the name of any of his toys?

      C.   Can he reach for an object and grasp it?

      D.   All of the above

Answer: D. All of the above.
Here are some characteristics of individuals with mental retardation or intellectual disabilities:

- IQ of 70 or below
- Limited cognitive ability; delayed academic achievement, particularly in language-related subjects
- Deficits in memory that often relate to poor initial perception or that relate to a poor inability to apply stored information to relevant situations
- Impaired formulation of learning strategies
- Difficulty in attending to relevant aspects of stimuli; slowness in reaction time or in employing alternate strategies.

2. **Which of the following statements about children with emotional/behavioral disorders is true?**
(Average) (Skill 1.1)

    A.   They have very high IQs.

    B.   They display poor social skills.

    C.   They are poor academic achievers.

    D.   Both B and C

Answer: D. Both B and C.
Children who exhibit mild behavioral disorders are characterized by:
- Average or above average scores on intelligence tests
- Poor academic achievement; learned helplessness
- Unsatisfactory interpersonal relationships
- Immaturity; attention seeking
- Aggressive, acting-out behavior, such as hitting, fighting, teasing, yelling, refusing to comply with requests, excessive attention seeking, poor anger control, temper tantrums, hostile reactions, and defiant use of language
- Anxious, withdrawn behavior, such as infantile behavior, social isolation, few friends, withdrawal into fantasy, fears, hypochondria, unhappiness, and crying

3. **Which behavior would be expected at the mild level of emotional/behavioral disorders?**
    (Rigorous) (Skill 1.1)

    A. Attention seeking

    B. Inappropriate affect

    C. Self-injurious actions

    D. Poor sense of identity

Answer: A. Attention seeking.
Children who exhibit mild behavioral disorders are characterized by:
- Average or above average scores on intelligence tests
- Poor academic achievement; learned helplessness
- Unsatisfactory interpersonal relationships
- Immaturity; attention seeking
- Aggressive, acting-out behavior, such as hitting, fighting, teasing, yelling, refusing to comply with requests, excessive attention seeking, poor anger control, temper tantrums, hostile reactions, and defiant use of language
- Anxious, withdrawn behavior, such as infantile behavior, social isolation, few friends, withdrawal into fantasy, fears, hypochondria, unhappiness, and crying

4. **Which category of behaviors would most likely be found on a behavior rating scale?**
    (Easy) (Skill 1.1)

    A. Disruptive, acting out

    B. Shy, withdrawn

    C. Aggressive (physical or verbal)

    D. All of the above

Answer: D. All of the above.
These are all possible problem behaviors that can adversely impact the student or the class, thus they may be found on behavior rating scales.

5.   **The social skills of students in mental retardation programs are likely to be appropriate for children of their mental age rather than chronological age. This means that the teacher will need to do all of the following except:**
(Easy) (Skill 1.1)

A.   Model desired behavior

B.   Provide clear instructions

C.   Expect age appropriate behaviors

D.   Adjust the physical environment when necessary

Answer: C. Expect age appropriate behaviors.
Age appropriate means mental age appropriate not chronological age appropriate.

6.   **Which of the following examples would be considered of highest priority when determining the need for the delivery of appropriate special education and related services?**
        (Rigorous) (Skill 1.1)

    A.   An eight-year-old boy is repeating first grade for the second time and exhibits problems with toileting, gross motor functions, and remembering number and letter symbols. His regular classroom teacher claims the referral forms are too time-consuming and refuses to complete them. The teacher also refuses to make accommodations because he feels every child should be treated alike.

    B.   A six-year-old girl who has been diagnosed as autistic is placed in a special education class within the local school. Her mother wants her to attend residential school next year, even though the girl is showing progress.

    C.   A ten-year-old girl with profound mental retardation is receiving education services in a state institution.

    D.   A twelve-year-old boy with mild disabilities is placed in a behavior disorders program but displays obvious perceptual deficits (e.g., reversal of letters and symbols, an inability to discriminate sounds). He was originally thought to have a learning disability but did not meet state criteria for this exceptionality category based on results of standard scores. He has always had problems with attending to tasks and is now beginning to get into trouble during seatwork time. His teacher feels that he will eventually become a real behavior problem. He receives social skills training in the resource room one period a day.

Answer: A. An eight-year-old boy is repeating first grade for the second time and exhibits problems with toileting, gross motor functions, and remembering number and letter symbols. His regular classroom teacher claims the referral forms are too time-consuming and refuses to complete them. The teacher also refuses to make accommodations because he feels every child should be treated alike.

No modifications are being made, so the child is not receiving any services whatsoever.

7.   The Carrow Elicited Language Inventory is a test designed to give the examiner diagnostic information about a child's expressive grammatical competence. Which of the following language components is being assessed?
(Rigorous) (Skill 1.1)

   A.   Phonology

   B.   Morphology

   C.   Syntax

   D.   Both B and C

Answer: C. Syntax
Although both morphology and syntax refer to understanding the grammatical structure of language in the receptive channel, as well as using the grammatical structure of language in the expressive channel, assessment of morphology refers to linguistic structure of words. Assessment of syntax includes grammatical usage of word classes, word order, and transformational rules for the variance of word order.

8.   In a Test of Psycholinguistic Abilities, the child is presented with a picture representing statements, such as the following: "Here is one die; here are two ____." This test is essentially a test of:
(Rigorous) (Skill 1.1)

   A.   Phonology

   B.   Morphology

   C.   Syntax

   D.   Semantics

Answer: C. Syntax
   • Phonology is the study of significant units of speech sounds.
   • Morphology is the study of the smallest units of language that convey meaning.
   • Syntax is a system of rules for making grammatically correct sentences.
   • Semantics is the study of the relationships between words and grammatical forms in a language, as well as the underlying meaning

9.   Five-year-old Tom continues to substitute the "w" sound for the "r" sound when pronouncing words; therefore, he often distorts words (e.g., "wabbit" for "rabbit" and "wat" for "rat"). His articulation disorder is basically a problem in:
      (Rigorous) (Skill 1.1)

      A.   Phonology

      B.   Morphology

      C.   Syntax

      D.   Semantics

Answer: A. Phonology
- Phonology is the study of significant units of speech sounds.
- Morphology is the study of the smallest units of language that convey meaning.
- Syntax is a system of rules for making grammatically correct sentences.
- Semantics is the study of the relationships between words and grammatical forms in a language, as well as the underlying meaning.

10.   Which of the following is untrue about the ending "er?"
      (Rigorous) (Skill 1.1)

      A.   It is an example of a free morpheme.

      B.   It represents one of the smallest units of meaning within a word.

      C.   It is called an inflectional ending.

      D.   When added to a word, it connotes a comparative status.

Answer: A. It is an example of a free morpheme.
Morpheme is the smallest unit of meaningful language. "Er" on its own has no meaning.

11. **Which component of language involves language content rather than the form of language?**
(Rigorous) (Skill 1.1)

    A.   Phonology

    B.   Morphology

    C.   Semantics

    D.   Syntax

Answer: C. Semantics
Semantics is the study of the relationships between words and grammatical forms in a language, as well as the underlying meaning.

12. **Which is least indicative of a developmental delay?**
(Rigorous) (Skill 1.1)

    A.   Language and speech production

    B.   Gross motor skills

    C.   Self-help skills

    D.   Arithmetic computation skills

Answer: D. Arithmetic computation skills
In a preschool environment, disabling conditions are manifested as the inability to learn adequate readiness skills; the inability to demonstrate self-help; and adaptive, social-interpersonal communication, or gross motor skills. The most typical symptoms exhibited by school-age students are inattention to tasks; disruptiveness; inability to learn to read, write, spell, or perform mathematical computations; unintelligible speech; an appearance of not being able to see or hear adequately; frequent daydreaming; excessive movement; and, in general, clumsiness and ineptitude in most school-related activities. Even though gross motor skills are exhibited in preschool children, they do not carry over to school-age children.

13. **A child with intellectual disabilities who is fairly clumsy and possesses poor social awareness—but who can be taught to communicate and to perform semiskilled labor and maintains himself under supervision—probably belongs to which level of classification as an adult?**
(Rigorous) (Skill 1.1)

    A.   Mild

    B.   Moderate

    C.   Severe

    D.   Profound

Answer: B. Moderate
Mild (IQ of 50–55 to 70)
- Delays in most areas (communication, motor, academic)
- Often not distinguished from normal children until of school age
- Can acquire both academic and vocational skills; can become self-supporting

Moderate (IQ of 35–40 to 50–55)
- Only fair motor development; clumsy
- Poor social awareness
- Can be taught to communicate
- Can profit from training in social and vocational skills; needs supervision but can perform semiskilled labor as an adult

14. **All of the following are common characteristics of a student who is emotionally disturbed *except*:**
(Average) (Skill 1.1)

    A.   Socially accepted by peers

    B.   Highly disruptive to the classroom environment

    C.   Academic difficulties

    D.   Areas of talent overlooked by a teacher

Answer: A. Socially accepted by peers
While a child may be socially accepted by peers, children who are emotionally disturbed tend to alienate those around them and are often ostracized.

15. **Duration is an appropriate measure to take with all of these behaviors EXCEPT:**
    (Easy) (Skill 1.2)

    A.   Thumb sucking

    B.   Hitting

    C.   Temper tantrums

    D.   Maintaining eye contact

Answer: B. Hitting
Hitting takes place in an instant. This should be measured by frequency.

16. **All children cry, hit, fight, and play alone, at different times. Children with behavior disorders will perform these behaviors at a higher than normal:**
    (Average) (Skill 1.2)

    A.   Rate

    B.   Topography

    C.   Duration

    D.   Magnitude

Answer: A. Rate
Rate describes how often a behavior occurs.

17. **Which of the following is typical of attention problems that a youngster with a learning disability might display?**
(Rigorous) (Skill 1.2)

    A.   Lack of selective attention

    B.   Does not consider consequences before acting

    C.   Unable to Control Own Actions or impulses

    D.   Poor fine motor coordination

Answer: A. Lack of selective attention
Here are some of the characteristics of persons with learning disabilities: Disorder in one or more basic psychological processes involved in understanding or in using spoken or written language that manifests itself in an imperfect ability to listen, think, speak, read, write, spell, or to do mathematical calculations. They cannot be attributed to visual, hearing, physical, intellectual, or emotional handicaps, or cultural, environmental, or economic disadvantage.

18. **Echolalia, repetitive stereotyped actions, and a severe disorder of thinking and communication are indicative of:**
(Rigorous) (Skill 1.2)

    A.   Psychosis

    B.   Schizophrenia

    C.   Autism

    D.   Paranoia

Answer: C. Autism
The behaviors listed are indicative of autism.

19. **In which of the following exceptionality categories may a student be considered for inclusion if his IQ score falls more than two standard deviations below the mean?**
    (Rigorous) (Skill 1.2)

    A. Mental Retardation

    B. Specific Learning Disabilities

    C. Emotionally/Behaviorally Disordered

    D. Gifted

Answer: A. Mental Retardation
Only about 1 to 1.5% of the population fit the AAMD's definition of mental retardation. They exhibit significantly subaverage general intellectual functioning with deficits in adaptive behavior, manifested during the developmental period, and adversely affecting educational performance.

20. **Individuals with mild mental retardation can be characterized as:**
    (Rigorous) (Skill 1.2)

    A. Often indistinguishable from normal developing children at an early age

    B. Having a higher than normal rate of motor activity

    C. Displaying significant discrepancies in ability levels

    D. Uneducable in academic skills

Answer: A. Often indistinguishable from normal developing children at an early age
See rationale of previous question.

21. **Which characteristic is *not* often present in children with profound multidisabilities?**
(Easy) (Skill 1.3)

   A.   Self-stimulation (rocking, hand-flapping)

   B.   Frequently nonambulatory

   C.   Excessively social and responsive to others

   D.   Aggressiveness toward others

Answer: C. Excessively social and responsive to others
Children with profound multidisabilities are often markedly withdrawn or unresponsive to others.

22. **Why must teachers maintain a positive attitude, and avoid bias?**
(Average) (Skill 2.4)

   A.   Positive attitudes enable a student to potentially believe in his or her abilities more.

   B.   Cultures and religions have different views.

   C.   Teaching is a calling; not a job.

   D.   Positivity provides optimism.

Answer: A. Positive attitudes enable a student to potentially believe in his or her abilities more.
Teachers have the responsibility to not allow their negative attitudes toward students to impact how they perceive the students interact with them. If the teacher is able to communicate to all of his or her students that they all have great potential and is optimistic regarding this, then the students should excel in some aspect of their educational endeavors. This continues to be true for as long as the teacher is able to make the student believe in him or herself.

23. **What type of medication is often used to treat depression and obsessive-compulsive behavior?**
   (Average) (Skill 2.5)

   A.   Oxidase inhibitors

   B.   Tricyclic antidepressants.

   C.   Selective serotonin-reuptake inhibitors

   D.   Stimulants

Answer: B. Tricyclic antidepressants.
A type of antidepressant is the tricyclic antidepressants. They are often effective for treating depression and obsessive-compulsive behavior. They cause similar side effects to the SSRIs, such as sedation, tremors, seizures, dry mouth, light sensitivity, and mood swings in students with bipolar disorders.

24. **Why must educators be aware of medication students may be taking?**
   (Rigorous) (Skill 2.5)

   A.   Medications can complicate curricular plans.

   B.   Many medications cause side effects.

   C.   Teachers can be more sensitive to the students' behaviors and attention spans.

   D.   All of the above

Answer: D. All of the above
If educators are aware of the types of medication that their students are taking, along with the myriad of side effects, they will be able to respond more positively when some of the side effects of the medication change their students' behaviors, response rates, and attention spans. Medical complications must be considered when developing schedules and curricular plans. Students may miss school due to medical conditions that require extensive rest or hospital-based intervention. Cooperative programs with home and hospital teachers can decrease the impact of such absences.

ASSESSING STUDENTS AND DEVELOPING PROGRAMS

25. **Which of the following is NOT an appropriate assessment modification or accommodation for a student with a learning disability?**
    (Average) (Skill 3.1)

    A.   Having the test read orally to the student

    B.   Writing down the student's dictated answers

    C.   Allowing the student to take the assessment home to complete

    D.   Extending the time for the student to take the assessment

Answer: C. Allowing the student to take the assessment home to complete
Unless a student is homebound, the student should take assessments in class or in another classroom setting. All the other items listed are appropriate accommodations.

26. **Children who write poorly might be given tests that allow oral responses unless the purpose for the test is to:**
    (Average) (Skill 3.1)

    A.   Assess handwriting skills

    B.   Test for organization of thoughts

    C.   Answer questions pertaining to math reasoning

    D.   Assess rote memory

Answer: A. Assess handwriting skills
It is necessary to have the child write if a teacher is assessing his or her skill in that domain.

28.   The purpose of error analysis of a test is to:
       (Easy) (Skill 3.1)

       A.   Determine what events were labeled in error

       B.   Determine if the test length was the cause of error

       C.   Evaluate the types of errors made by categorizing incorrect answers

       D.   Establish a baseline

Answer: C. Evaluate the types of errors made by categorizing incorrect answers
Error analysis examines how and why a person makes a mistake. In an informal reading inventory, for example, questions are given to specifically address possible errors. A math assessment might provide a selection of answers on a multiple choice test that pinpoint whether the error is due failure to understand place value, failure to regroup, or failure to remember basic addition facts, etc. Other tests that utilize error analysis provide specific possible answers to denote which error was made. The purpose of both is to see where problems lie and to provide clues to assist the learning process.

28.   You are working with a functional program and have placed a student in a vocational position in the kitchen of a coffee house. A waiter takes orders and relays them to the student, whose job is to make the coffee as ordered. You need to perform a task analysis of making a cup of coffee. Which task should be first in the analysis?
       (Average) (Skill 3.1)

       A.   Filling the pot with water

       B.   Taking the order

       C.   Measuring the coffee

       D.   Picking the correct coffee

Answer: D. Picking the correct coffee
While the student is in a coffee house, the task was to make coffee, not to wait on customers. There are different kinds of coffee (decaffeinated, regular, etc.) and they all have their appropriate canisters. The student must be able to choose the correct coffee before measuring it.

29.   **How are informal assessments quantified and measured?**
       (Average) (Skill 3.1)

      A.   Via observational notes

      B.   They cannot be quantified

      C.   Decile scoring

      D.   Percentile ranking

Answer: A. Via observational notes
Although at times informal assessments do not have to be quantified, they can be easily scored. Anecdotal records and observational logs can be filled out, and interviewing or informal questioning is an efficient way to record results.

30.   **Standardized tests allow:**
       (Easy) (Skill 3.1)

      A.   Administration to groups

      B.   Administration to individuals

      C.   Comparison across population

      D.   All of the above

Answer: D. All of the above
Standardized tests are flexible and allow several types of comparisons to be made. Comparisons across populations, ages, genders, grades, and so forth can be made.

31.   **What are individual intelligence tests used for primarily?**
      (Average) (Skill 3.1)

      A.   Program placement in a classroom

      B.   Classification

      C.   Defining a person's potential

      D.   Screening groups

Answer: B. Classification
Individual intelligence tests are used to classify individuals. Often results are reflected in IEPs and similar legal documents to demonstrate the intelligence level of the individual. Newer types of testing are being put into practice, such as Howard Gardener's Multiple Intelligences.

32.   **Formal assessments include standardized tests, norm-referenced Instruments, and:**
      (Rigorous) (Skill 3.1)

      A.   Developmental rating scales

      B.   Interviews

      C.   Anecdotes/ Observations

      D.   Textbook chapter tests

Answer: D. Textbook chapter tests
Formal assessments are assessments such as standardized tests or textbook quizzes; objective tests that include primarily questions for which there is only one correct, easily identifiable answer. These can be commercial or teacher made assessments. *Informal* assessments have less objective measures, and may include anecdotes or observations that may or may not be quantified, interviews, informal questioning during a task, etc.

33. **Which of the following is an advantage of giving informal individual assessments, rather than standardized group tests?**
(Easy) (Skill 3.1)

   A.   Questions can be modified to reveal a specific student's strategies or misconceptions.

   B.   The test administrator can clarify or rephrase questions for the student.

   C.   They can be inserted into the class quickly on an as needed basis.

   D.   All of the above

Answer: D. All of the above
Standardized group tests are administered to a group in a specifically prescribed manner, with strict rules to keep procedures, scoring, and interpretation of results uniform in all cases. Such tests allow comparisons to be made across populations, ages or grades. *Informal* assessments have less objective measures, and may include anecdotes or observations that may or may not be quantified, interviews, informal questioning during a task, etc. An example of an informal *individually* administered assessment might be watching a student sort objects to see what attribute is most important to the student, or questioning a student to see what he or she found confusing about a task.

34. **Criterion referenced tests can provide information about:**
(Rigorous) (Skill 3.1)

   A.   Whether a student has mastered prerequisite skills

   B.   Whether a student is ready to proceed to the next level of instruction

   C.   Which instructional materials might be helpful in covering program objectives

   D.   All of the above

Answer: A. Whether a student has mastered prerequisite skills
In criterion referenced testing, the emphasis is on assessing specific and relevant skills or knowledge bases that have been mastered. Items on criterion-referenced tests are often linked directly to specific instructional objectives.

35.   **The extent to which a test measures what it claims to measure is called:**
      (Rigorous) (Skill 3.2)

      A.   Reliability

      B.   Validity

      C.   Factor analysis

      D.   Chi Square

Answer: B. Validity
Validity is defined as the degree to which a test measures is what it claims to measure. There are several kids of validity, such as content validity, construct validity and predictive validity.

36.   **Acculturation refers to the individual's:**
      (Rigorous) (Skill 3.3)

      A.   Gender

      B.   Experiential background

      C.   Social class

      D.   Ethnic background

Answer: B. Experiential background
Acculturation is differences in experiential background. A person's culture has little to do with gender, social class, or ethnicity. A person is the product of his or her experiences.

37. **What type of data does a teacher organize and prepare for student evaluations?**
(Average) (Skill 4.1)

    A.   Reason for assessment

    B.   Test results

    C.   Educational Recommendations

    D.   All of the above

Answer: D. All of the above
Although the school psychologist often completes student evaluations and writes a report, this may be the task of the special educator when assessment is done in the classroom in preparation for the student's annual review. In this case, the special education teacher will be asked to write a report summarizing assessment findings and educational implications. The teacher should be able to organize the data in a concise, readable format. Some components of such a report include the following:
- Identifying information (student name, age, date of birth, address, gender)
- Reason for assessment
- Test administration information (date, time, duration of test, response of student)
- Test results
- Summary of educational recommendations

38. **What is the purpose of teacher assistance teams?**
(Average) (Skill 4.2)

    A.   Make professional suggestions

    B.   Recommend instructional modifications

    C.   Offer curricular alternatives

    D.   All of the above

Answer: D. All of the above
Chalfant, Pysh, and Moultrie (1979) state that **teacher assistance teams** are created to make professional suggestions about curricular alternatives and instructional modifications. These teams may be composed of a variety of participants, including regular education teachers, building administrators, guidance counselors, special education teachers, and the student's parent(s). The team composition varies based on the type of referral, the needs of the student, and availability of educational personnel and state requirements.

39. **Why provide a student with a checklist or check sheet?**
(Average) (Skill 4.2)

    A.   Students cannot track their accomplishments.

    B.   Check sheets are markers of success.

    C.   Checklists provide loose structure.

    D.   Check sheets relate material that is relevant to the student.

Answer: B. Check sheets are markers of success.
Students with learning problems need frequent reinforcement for their efforts. Charts, graphs, and check sheets provide tangible markers of student achievement.

40. **Why should teachers use a variety of assessment techniques?**
(Easy) (Skill 4.3)

    A.   To understand the benefits of assessments

    B.   To determine the existing knowledge, skills, needs

    C.   To offer numerical data to state regulatory agencies

    D.   All of the above

Answer: B. To determine the existing knowledge, skills, and needs
Assessment is the key to providing differentiated and appropriate instruction to all students, and this is the area in which teachers will most often use assessment. Teachers should use a variety of assessment techniques to determine the existing knowledge, skills, and needs of each student. Depending on the age of the student and the subject matter under consideration, diagnosis of readiness may be accomplished through pretest, checklists, teacher observation, or student self-report.

41. **What is the purpose of diagnosis via assessment?**
    (Average) (Skill 4.3)

     A. To identify students who are not ready for new material

     B. To scan the classroom for additional data

     C. To find students who can answer all questions

     D. To understand the classroom as a whole

Answer: A. To identify students who are not ready for new material
Diagnosis serves two related purposes—to identify those students who are not ready for the new instruction and to identify for each student what prerequisite knowledge is lacking. Student assessment is an integral part of the teaching-learning process. Identifying student, teacher, or program weaknesses is only significant if the information so obtained is used to remedy those concerns.

42. **What is the ultimate goal of diagnostic endeavors?**
    (Average) (Skill 4.3)

     A. Find students who do well

     B. Create tests

     C. Gather data on certain topics

     D. Improve learning

Answer: D. Improve learning
Lesson materials and lesson delivery must be evaluated to determine relevant prerequisite skills and abilities. The teacher must be capable of determining whether a student's difficulties lie with the new information, with a lack of significant prior knowledge, or with a core learning disability that must be addressed with specialized lesson plans or accommodations. The ultimate goal of any diagnostic or assessment endeavor is improved learning. Thus, instruction is adapted to the needs of the learner based on assessment information.

43. **How should assessment information be used?**
(Average) (Skill 4.3)

    A.   To provide performance-based criteria

    B.   To set academic expectations

    C.   To identify areas of weakness

    D.   All of the above

Answer: D. All of the above
Assessment skills should be an integral part of teacher training. Teachers are able to use pre- and post-assessments of content areas to monitor student learning, analyze assessment data in terms of individualized support for students and instructional practice for teachers, and design lesson plans that have measurable outcomes and definitive learning standards. Assessment information should be used to provide performance-based criteria and academic expectations for all students in evaluating whether students have learned the expected skills and content of the subject area.

44. **Why is it important that teachers make inferences?**
(Rigorous) (Skill 4.3)

    A.   Teachers can verify factual data.

    B.   They can guess why a student is struggling.

    C.   They can gather definitive information about projected student performance.

    D.   They can learn about the students.

Answer: C. They can gather definitive information about projected student performance.
By making inferences on teaching methods and gathering clues for student performance, teachers can use assessment data to inform and have an impact on instructional practices. By analyzing the various types of assessments, teachers can gather more definitive information on projected student academic performance. Instructional strategies for teachers would provide learning targets for student behavior, cognitive thinking skills, and processing skills that can be employed to diversify student learning opportunities.

45. **How should intelligence test scores be interpreted?**
(Rigorous) (Skill 4.3)

A.   In terms of the person's potential

B.   In terms of the class potential

C.   In terms of performance

D.   In terms of test reliability

Answer: C. In terms of performance
Particular care must be taken in interpreting some tests. Intelligence test scores, for example, should be interpreted in terms of performance and not the person's potential.

46. **Which terms should a teacher become familiar with when conducting and interpreting tests?**
(Average) (Skill 4.3)

   A.   Standardized information

   B.   Relativity to the student population

   C.   Interpretation of charts and graphs

   D.   All of the above

Answer: D. All of the above
The teacher must read the test manuals and become familiar with the following items:

- Areas measured: Verbal, quantitative, memory, cognitive skills, or the multiple intelligences on some assessments.
- Population: Target age groups, lack of cultural bias, adaptations or norms for children with physical handicaps such as blindness.
- Standardization information: Mean and standard deviation, scaled scores and what they mean.
- Means of comparing performance among subtests, such as the Verbal and Performance IQ scores of the WISC-IV
- Uses of the results: The test manual will contain information about how the results can be used (e.g., using the K-ABC-II to identify gifted children), or how they are not to be used (e.g., assuming that a 3rd grade student who gets a score like a 5th grader on a 3rd grade test is ready to do 5th grade work, an assumption that would not be correct).
- Information on use with special populations, such as Spanish-speaking students, students with visual impairments, physical impairments, or learning disabilities.
- Information concerning reliability and validity.

47. **Which of the following purposes of testing calls for an informal test? (Rigorous) (Skill 4.3)**

   A. Screening a group of children to determine their readiness for the first reader

   B. Analyzing the responses of a student with a disability to various presentations of content material to see which strategy works for him

   C. Evaluating the effectiveness of a fourth-grade math program at the end of its first year of use in a specific school

   D. Determining the general level of intellectual functioning of a class of fifth graders

Answer: B. Analyzing the responses of a student with disability to various presentations of content material to see which strategy works for him
Formal tests such as standardized tests or textbook quizzes are objective tests that include primarily questions for which there is only one correct answer. Some are teacher prepared, but they are often commercially prepared and frequently standardized. To analyze the response of a student to types of presentation, informal methods such as observation or questioning are more useful.

48. **A transition or vocational curriculum approach focuses on: (Rigorous) (Skill 4.4)**

   A. Remediation of basic academic skills

   B. Preparation for functioning in society as adults

   C. Preparation for the world of work

   D. Daily living and social skills

Answer: B. Preparation for functioning in society as adults
A transition or vocational curriculum approach focuses upon what students need to learn that will be useful to them and prepare them for functioning in society as adults. Life preparation includes not only occupational readiness, but also personal-social, and daily living skills.

49. **Which of the following is an important principle when a student is transitioning from one program or setting to another?**
    (Average) (Skill 4.4)

    A. Services should be interrupted temporarily until new services are available in the new setting.

    B. Transition should include duplication in assessment and goal planning.

    C. All student records should be transferred to the new setting so that no ongoing communication is necessary.

    D. Transition should be viewed as a process.

Answer: D. Transition should be viewed as a process.
To help all parties experience success in the new setting, transition should be viewed as a process. Transition should be marked by ongoing communication and collaborative partnerships.

50. **Transition planning should involve all of the following except**
    (Easy) (Skill 4.4)

    A. Service coordinators

    B. Families

    C. Other students

    D. Teachers

Answer: C. Other students
Participants in the transition process include children and their families, service coordinators, early childhood special educators, related services practitioners, administrators, and others involved in the child's transition.

51. **What is the purpose of keeping student portfolios?**
   (Average) (Skill 4.5)

   A.   Compile student work

   B.   Monitor progress over a period of time

   C.   Presentation for parent-teacher conference

   D.   All of the above

Answer: D. All of the above
Student portfolios provide a wealth of information, as well as insight into the student's progression in a particular subject. They serve as a great assessment tool and show samples of the student's understanding of various topics.

PROMOTING STUDENT DEVELOPMENT AND LEARNING

52. **What is one way to differentiate the class in a large group setting?**
   (Average) (Skill 5.1)

   A.   Modify instruction time

   B.   Avoid visual aids

   C.   Do not allow breaks

   D.   Establish a rule

Answer: A. modify instruction time
Keep instruction shorter for first grade to seventh grade, ranging from five to fifteen minutes. Allow students to stretch to keep alert, and use lecture-pause routines. Always ask questions that involve all students.

53. **Who determines peer tutoring goals?**
(Average) (Skill 5.1)

    A.   Peers

    B.   IEP team

    C.   Teachers

    D.   Consultant teachers

Answer: C. Teachers
Although input from all choices is relevant, the teacher should determine the target goals and select the material to be presented. The teacher is also required to monitor progress and evaluate the sessions.

54. **Which type of grouping arrangement would be MOST effective for teaching basic academic skills such as math facts or reading?**
(Rigorous) (Skill 5.1)

    A.   Large group with teacher

    B.   Peer tutoring

    C.   Small group instruction

    D.   Cooperative learning

Answer: C. Small group instruction
Small group instruction usually includes five to seven students and is recommended for teaching basic academic skills such as math facts or reading. This model is especially effective for students with learning problems. Large-group instruction is time efficient and prepares students for higher levels of secondary and post-secondary education settings. However, with large groups, instruction cannot be as easily tailored to high or low levels of students. Peer tutoring is not appropriate for teaching basic concepts. Peer tutoring can be effective in practice and review where the teacher trains the peer tutors and matches them with students who need extra practice and assistance. Cooperative learning differs from peer tutoring in that students are grouped in teams or small groups, and the methods are based on teamwork, individual accountability, and team reward. This approach is appropriate for discovery type lessons, rather than specific instruction in introductory concepts.

55.   How is student motivation increased when classroom instruction is modified?
(Average) (Skill 5.2)

A.   Students can manipulate materials that they use in their lives.

B.   Students can practice new skills.

C.   Students can process material easier.

D.   Information is relevant to the student.

Answer: A. Students can manipulate materials that they use in their lives.
Active learning experiences teach concepts that motivate students. The students can manipulate, weigh, measure, read, or write using materials and skills that relate to their daily lives.

56.   Teaching techniques that stimulate active participation and understanding in the mathematics class include all but which of the following?
(Easy) (Skill 5.2)

A.   Having students copy computation facts for a set number of times.

B.   Asking students to find the error in an algorithm.

C.   Giving immediate feedback to students.

D.   Having students chart their progress.

Answer: A. Having students copy computation facts for a set number of times
Copying does not stimulate participation or understanding.

57. **The social skills of students with mental retardation disabilities are likely to be appropriate for children of their mental age, rather than chronological age. This means that the teacher whose class contains children with these disabilities will need to do all of the following except:**
(Easy) (Skill 5.2)

A. Model desired behavior

B. Provide clear instructions

C. Expect age appropriate behaviors

D. Adjust the physical environment when necessary

Answer: C. Expect age appropriate behaviors
Age appropriate in this example refers to the student's mental age or functioning level, not his/her chronological age.

58. **Modifications in the classroom include which of the following:**
(Average) (Skill 5.2)

A. Reduced number of spelling words on the weekly quiz

B. Highlighting and clarifying directions

C. Providing a word bank

D. All of the above

Answer: D All of the above.
Modifications that may be considered for the general education classroom include the amount of work or type of task required. Modifications for a student with a learning disability might include a reduced number of spelling words or a task of writing the vocabulary word that goes with a given definition instead of writing the definition that goes with a given word.

59. All of the following are suggestions for *pacing* or altering the presentation of tasks to match the student's rate of learning except: *(Average) (Skill 5.3)*

    A.   Teach in several shorter segments of time rather than a single lengthy session

    B.   Continue to teach a task until the lesson is completed in order to provide more time on task

    C.   Watch for nonverbal cues that indicate students are becoming confused, bored, or restless

    D.   Avoid giving students an inappropriate amount of written work

Answer: B. Continue to teach a task until the lesson is completed in order to provide more time on task

This action does not alter the subject content; neither does it alter the rate at which tasks are presented. Pacing is the term used for altering of tasks to match the student's rate of learning. This can be done in two ways: altering the subject content and the rate at which tasks are presented. However, both methods require adjusting presentation based on the child's performance along the way, and introducing a new task only when the student has demonstrated mastery of the previous task in the learning hierarchy.

60. The rule is "no talking during silent reading time." Mrs. Jenkins gives her students 20 minutes each Friday to quietly read a book or magazine of their choice. And every Friday, Karl turns to talk to Jake. What non-aversive technique may Mrs. Jenkins employ to reduce this undesirable behavior?
(Rigorous) (Skill 5.3)

    A.   Self-assessment

    B.   Planned ignoring

    C.   Proximity control

    D.   Token economy

Answer: C. Proximity control

Mrs. Jenkins can reduce the talking simply by stepping in Karl's direction. This signal can inhibit the extraneous talking, and encourage Karl to be on task, and not distract Jake, or the other students who may need absolute silence to focus.

61.   **How can a teacher decide when rules are broken or complied with?**
       (Average) (Skill 5.3)

       A.   A system of positive consequences, or rewards, can promote a positive classroom.

       B.   Positive expectations give the teacher an assertive response style

       C.   Setting limits allows students to refrain from negative behavior.

       D.   All of the above.

Answer: D. All of the above.
Teachers must have sense of control in the classroom. Merely making rules is not enough to reinforce classroom expectations. Systems of consequences and rewards, limits, and assertive response styles all contribute to the classroom agenda.

62.   **When developing a management plan, teachers must be:**
       (Average) (Skill 5.3)

       A.   Focused on reward systems

       B.   Open to students dictating the rules

       C.   Proactive

       D.   Sole developer of rationale

Answer: C. Proactive.
Although student-produced rules are welcomed, positive procedures and behavior management techniques should also be shaped to curb possible problems, and reflect what behaviors are expected of the class.

63. **In establishing a classroom behavior management plan with the students, it is best to:**
(Average) (Skill 5.3)

A.   Have rules written and in place on day one

B.   Hand out a copy of the rules to the students on day one

C.   Have separate rules for each class on day one

D.   Have students involved in creating the rules on day one

Answer: D. Have students involved in creating the rules on day one
Rules are easier to follow when students not only know the reason they are in place, but they took part in creating them. It may be good to already have a few rules pre-written and then to discuss if they cover all the rules the students have created. If not, it is possible you may want to modify your set of pre-written rules.

64. **Laura is beginning to raise her hand first instead of talking out. An effective schedule of reinforcement should be:**
(Average) (Skill 5.3)

A.   Continuous

B.   Variable

C.   Intermittent

D.   Fixed

Answer: A. Continuous
Note that the behavior is new. The pattern of reinforcement should not be variable, intermittent, or fixed. Continuous reinforcement is most effective at establishing new behaviors.

65.   **Which of the following is NOT a feature of effective classroom rules?** *(Easy) (Skill 5.3)*

      A.   They are about four to six in number

      B.   They are negatively stated

      C.   Consequences are consistent and immediate

      D.   They can be tailored to individual teaching goals and teaching styles

Answer B: They are negatively stated
Rules should be positively stated to encourage positive feedback.

66.   **What is *not* an example of the use of a punishment procedure?** *(Rigorous) (Skill 5.3)*

      A.   Ted quit talking with Jim when Mrs. Green frowned at him.

      B.   Timmy stopped getting out of his seat when the teacher scolded him.

      C.   Mary completed her math when her teacher told her she would have to miss recess if she wasn't through with the work.

      D.   Fred stopped making funny faces when Mrs. Smith placed him in time out.

Answer: C.
A punisher is a consequential stimulus, which has the following characteristics:
- It decreases the future rate or probability of the occurrence of the behavior.
- It is administered contingent on the production of an undesired behavior.
- It is administered immediately following the production of the undesired behavior.

In "C," Mary received a prompt, not a consequential stimulus.

67.	Mr. Smith is on a field trip with a group of high school EH students. On the way, they stop at a fast-food restaurant for lunch, and Warren and Raul get into an argument. After some heated words, Warren stalks out of the restaurant and refuses to return to the group. He leaves the parking lot, continues walking away from the group, and ignores Mr. Smith's directions to come back. What would be the best course of action for Mr. Smith?
(Rigorous) (Skill 5.4)

  A.	Leave the group with the class aide and follow Warren to try to talk him into coming back

  B.	Wait a little while and see if Warren cools off and returns

  C.	Telephone the school and let the crisis teacher notify the police in accordance with school policy

  D.	Call the police himself

Answer: C. Telephone the school and let the crisis teacher notify the police in accordance with school policy
Mr. Smith is still responsible for his class. He cannot leave the entire class with the aide. His school should have a policy in place for such situations. This is his best option.

68.	**What are organizers?**
(Easy) (Skill 6.1)

  A.	Learning tools

  B.	Visual aids

  C.	Diagrams

  D.	All of the above

Answer: D. all of the above
Visual aids, such as organizers, or graphics, including diagrams, tables, charts, and guides, alert the students to the nature and content of the lesson.

69. **To facilitate learning instructional objectives:**
    (Average) (Skill 6.1)

    A. They should be taken from a grade-level spelling list

    B. They should be written and shared

    C. They should be arranged in order of similarity

    D. They should be taken from a scope and sequence

Answer C: They should be arranged in order of similarity
To facilitate learning, instructional objectives should be arranged in order according to their patterns of similarity. Objectives involving similar responses should be closely sequenced; thus, the possibility for positive transfer is stressed.

70. **Which of the following is a good example of a generalization?**
    (Average) (Skill 6.1)

    A. Jim has learned to add and is now ready to subtract

    B. Sarah adds sets of units to obtain a product

    C. Bill recognizes a vocabulary word on a billboard when traveling

    D. Jane can spell the word "net" backwards to get the word "ten"

Answer: C. Bill recognizes a vocabulary word on a billboard when traveling
Generalization is the occurrence of a learned behavior in the presence of a stimulus other than the one that produced the initial response. Students must be able to expand or transfer what is learned to other settings (e.g., reading to math word problems, resource room to regular classroom). Transfer of learning can be positive or negative. Positive transfer occurs when elements of what is learned on one task are also applicable to a new task, so the second task is easier to learn. Negative transfer occurs when elements of what was learned on one task interfere with what needs to be learned on a new task.

71.   John learns best through the auditory channel, so his teacher wants to reinforce his listening skills. Through which of the following types of equipment would instruction be most effectively presented?
(Easy) (Skill 6.2)

      A.   Overhead Projector

      B.   CD Player

      C.   Microcomputer

      D.   Opaque Projector

Answer: B. CD Player
As he is an auditory learner, the ability to listen to information would help sharpen and further develop John's listening skills.

72.   What Assistive Technology (AT) is best for Bob, who can compose well, but has difficulty with both encoding and the physical act of writing?
(Average) (Skill 6.2)

      A.   A peer to write what he dictates

      B.   Voice to text computer software

      C.   A CD player he can listen to while others write

      D.   A slant board for writing

Answer: B. Voice to text computer software
Voice to text computer software is ideal for a student who can compose well (written expression), but who cannot *write down* his thoughts either because he cannot encode (spell) adequately or because he has a physical disability that makes the physical act of writing difficult. The computer allows him to focus on his expression without worrying about physical mechanics. Dictating to a teacher or a peer will also work, but these are not forms of AT. Listening to a CD while others write is not access to the curriculum.

73. **When a student begins to use assistive technology, it is important for the teacher to have a clear outline as to when and how the equipment should be used. Why?**
(Rigorous) (Skill 6.2)

    A.   To establish a level of accountability with the student.

    B.   To establish that the teacher has responsibility for the equipment that is in use in his or her room.

    C.   To establish that the teacher is responsible for the usage of the assistive technology.

    D.   To establish a guideline for evaluation.

Answer A: To establish a level of accountability with the student
Establishing clear parameters as to the usage of assistive technology in a classroom creates a level of accountability in the student. The student will know that the teacher understands the intended purpose and appropriate use of the device and expects the student to do so, as well.

74. **What criteria must be considered when choosing assistive technology (AT) to help a particular student?**
(Easy) (Skill 6.2)

    A.   Whether there is a specific need the AT can meet (e.g., a goal on the IEP that requires it)

    B.   The degree of independence with which the student can use the device

    C.   The need for collaborative planning for the device to be used across all relevant settings and transfer between settings

    D.   All of the above

Answer: D. All of the above
In addition to the above, it is also necessary to consider: the amount of training the student and staff will need with the device, the specific contexts in which the device will be used (e.g., a language board might be used in all settings, but a computer program might only be used in writing), the plan for transitions and storage.

75. **There are several types of AT devices. They include:** *(Rigorous) (Skill 6.2)*

    A.   Graphic Organizers

    B.   Hearing Aides

    C.   Handwritten Notes

    D.   Supply Cases

Answer: B. Hearing Aides.
IDEA provides the following definition of an **Assistive Technology device**:
"Any item, piece of equipment or product system, whether acquired commercially off the shelf, modified, or customized that is used to increase, maintain or improve functional capabilities of children with disabilities." Choices A, C, and D, are learning tools or modifications.

76. **Learning tools are offered in both low-tech and high-tech options. What can be used for math class?**
(Average) (Skill 6.2)

    A. Notebook paper

    B. Manipulatives

    C. Text books

    D. Lab tables

Answer: B. Manipulatives.
To support students with difficulties in math, both low tech and high tech options are available.

- *Calculators*: Students who have difficulty performing math calculations can benefit from the use of a calculator. Adapted calculators may have larger buttons or larger display screens that are useful for students with physical disabilities. Talking calculators are available for students with visual impairments.
- *On-Screen Electronic Worksheets:* For student with physical disabilities who have difficulty with writing, worksheets can be produced in an on-screen format, allowing the student to use a computer screen to answer the questions.
- *Manipulatives of all types:* Students who have difficulty acquiring or retaining math concepts often benefit from objects designed to provide a kinesthetic or visual illustration of the concept. These low tech aids include such things as place value blocks, fraction strips, geared clocks, play money, etc.

WORKING IN A PROFESSIONAL ENVIRONMENT

77. **What made the Smith v. Robinson (1984) case significant?**
(Rigorous) (Skill 7.1)

    A.   Attorney's fees would be paid to parents who won litigation.

    B.   Students could not be denied an education due to behavior

    C.   Specific health services became mandated

    D.   "Free and Public" Education was established.

Answer: A. Attorney's fees would be paid to parents who won litigation.
This case concerned reimbursement of attorney's fees for parents who win litigation under IDEA. At the time of this case, IDEA did not provide for such reimbursement. Following this ruling, Congress passed a law awarding attorney's fees to parents who win their litigation.

78. **One of the most important goals of the special education teacher is to foster and create with the student:**
(Easy) (Skill 7.1)

    A.   Handwriting skills

    B.   Self-advocacy

    C   An increased level of reading

    D.   Logical reasoning

Answer: B. Self-advocacy
When a student achieves the ability to recognize his/her deficits and knows how to correctly advocate for his/her needs, the child has learned one of the most important life skills.

79. **Greg is a three-year-old boy who has recently survived a bout of meningitis. The pediatrician who treated Greg during his illness had to inform Greg's parents about some brain dysfunction which he had medically diagnosed. A reaction which would be anticipated upon learning of Greg's condition is:**
(Easy) (Skill 7.1)

   A.   Shock

   B.   Disbelief

   C.   Denial

   D.   All of the Above

Answer: D. All of the above
Although reactions are unique to individuals, the first emotions generally felt by the parents or guardians of a child with disabilities is shock, followed by disbelief, guilt, rejection, shame, denial and helplessness. As caregivers finally accept the reality of their child's condition, many report feeling anxiety or fear of their inability to care for the child. Many will doctor shop, hoping to find answers. Others will reject or refuse to believe information given by health care professionals.

80. **Early 19th century is considered a period of great importance in the field of special education because principles presently used in working with exceptional students were formulated by Itard. These principles included:**
(Average) (Skill 7.1)

   A.   Individualized instruction

   B.   Sequence of tasks

   C.   Functional life-like skills curriculum

   D.   All of the above

Answer: D. All of the above
A French Physician, Jean Marc Itard, had found a boy abandoned in the woods of Aveyron, France. His attempts to civilize and educate the boy, Victor, established these principles, including developmental and multisensory approaches. At that time, students with mild intellectual sensory impairments, mild intellectual disabilities, and emotional disorders were referred to as 'idiotic' and 'insane'.

81.   **Acceptance of disabilities by parents and siblings is most influenced by:**
        (Rigorous) (Skill 7.1)

        A.   Students obtain career training from elementary through high school

        B.   Students acquire specific training in job skills prior to exiting school

        C.   Students need specific training and supervision in applying skills learned in school to requirements in job situations

        D.   Students obtain needed instruction and field-based experiences that help them to be able to work in specific occupations

Answer: C. Students need specific training and supervision in applying skills learned in school to requirements in job situations
The cultural influence on the family has the largest impact on their understanding of the disability.

82.   **Students with disabilities develop greater self-images and recognize their own academic and social strengths when they are:**
        (Easy) (Skill 7.1)

        A.   Included in the mainstream classroom

        B.   Provided community based internships

        C.   Socializing in the hallway

        D.   Provided 1:1 instructional opportunity

Answer: A. Included in the mainstream classroom
When a child with a disability is included in the regular classroom it raises the expectations of the child's academic performance and their need to conform to "acceptable peer behavior." These expectations can help the child succeed, assuming he/she has the capacity to do so in that setting. Care should be taken, however, not to expect a child to succeed in a setting that is not appropriate for him/her.

83. **Society has normalized views toward those who are physically disabled by:**
(Easy) (Skill 7.1)

   A.   Providing normal living arrangements

   B.   Offering access to public facilities

   C.   Making improvements in the media

   D.   All of the above

Answer: D. All of the above.
American society has move from the method of institutionalization for that of normalization. Houses in local communities are often purchased for the purpose of providing supervision and/or nursing care that allow people with disabilities to have normal social living arrangements. Congress passed laws that allow those with disabilities to access public facilities. Public facilities have widened doorways, added special bathrooms, and made other architectural adjustments. America's media today provides education and frequent exposure to people with special needs.

84. **Which of the following must be completed before comprehensive testing occurs?**
(Average) (Skill 7.2)

   A.   Teacher consult on student needs

   B.   Pre-CSE conference

   C.   Parental permission for each test

   D.   All of the above

Answer: C. Parental permission for each test
The only piece required by both Part 200 and IDEA 2004 is parental permission for each test.

85. **What does Zero Reject require for all children with disabilities?**
   (Rigorous) (Skill 7.2)

     A.   Full inclusion of ALL students with disabilities in regular education classrooms and reporting annually

     B.   Seeking out and providing services to ALL students with disabilities regardless of type or severity and reporting annually

     C.   Free, appropriate public education provided to ALL students

     D.   Both B and C

Answer: D. Both B and C
The principle of Zero Reject requires that all children with disabilities be provided with a free, appropriate public education regardless of the type or severity of the disability. It also requires that states have procedures to *seek out* and identify students in need of services through effective outreach programs. The LEA reporting procedure locates, identifies, and evaluates children with disabilities within a given jurisdiction to ensure their attendance in public school and reports on these efforts annually. Zero Reject does NOT mean all will be served in full inclusion.

86. **How can a school violate the IDEA law?**
   (Average) (Skill 7.2)

     A.   The school fails to adequately search for students with disabilities.

     B.   The school takes too long identifying and providing services to a child.

     C.   The school fails to provide services listed in the IEP.

     D.   All of the above

Answer: D. All of the above.
Any school system, school, or teacher violating IDEA law can be held legally accountable. "Violating IDEA" can mean many different things. School systems can be found in violation if they fail to adequately search for students with disabilities, if they take too long to identify and provide services to a child, or if they fail to provide services listed in the IEP, among other things.

87. **How can a teacher violate the IDEA law?**
    (Rigorous) (Skill 7.2)

    A. A teacher does not provide modifications required by the IEP.

    B. A teacher teaches in one style and does not differentiate.

    C. A teacher does not utilize and work in conjunction with the paraprofessional staff accordingly.

    D. A teacher does not utilize the technology in the room, i.e. Smartboard.

Answer: A. A teacher does not provide modifications required by the IEP.
When teachers are found in violation, it is usually because they have failed to provide the modifications and accommodations required by a student's IEP. All such "violations" mean, basically, that a student's rights have been violated, that something a school or teacher did or did NOT do deprived a student of the right to FAPE or LRE.

88. **According to IDEA 2004, students with disabilities are to do what?**
    (Rigorous) (Skill 7.2)

    A. Participate in the general education program to the fullest extent that it is beneficial for them

    B. Participate in a vocational training program within the general education setting

    C. Participate in a general education program for physical education

    D. Participate in a Full Inclusion program that meets their needs

Answer: A. Participate in the general education program to the fullest extent that it is beneficial for them
The term "full inclusion" is not used in IDEA or federal statutes. IDEA requires that students be included in the least restrictive environment that meets their needs. It states that this environment should be as close to that experienced by students without disabilities as is practical, but also states that not all students can benefit from full participation in general education classrooms, and school systems must provide for all levels of placement. This can mean that a particular student's LRE may restrict him or her to a substantially separate program for the entire school day, but it should be possible to meet most students' needs in a less restrictive setting. Choices B, C, and D are all examples of possible settings related to participating in the general education setting to the fullest extent possible.

89. **Jacob's mother describes him as her "little leader." He organizes games at home, takes responsibility for setting the table, and initiates play. She states that her other, younger son is more of a follower; he is aloof and does not seem to stand up for himself. This demonstrates:**
(Average) (Skill 8.1)

   A.   Triangles

   B.   Sibling Position

   C.   Nuclear Family Emotional System

   D.   Family Projection Process

Answer: B. Sibling Position
Sibling Position is when birth order reflects tendencies of children in later interactions. Firstborn children tend to be leaders; younger siblings tend to be followers.

90. **All of the following are essential components of effective parent-teacher conferences EXCEPT:**
(Easy) (Skill 8.2)

   A.   Collecting samples of student work, records of behavior, and other relevant information

   B.   Beginning the conference with positive comments about the student

   C.   Using informal small talk to put the parents at ease

   D.   Preparing a list of questions or concerns you wish to address

Answer: C. Using informal small talk to put the parents at ease
While you do want to begin the conference by putting the parents at ease and by taking the time to establish a comfortable mood, you should not waste time with unnecessary small talk. Begin your discussion with positive comments about the student, and be polite and professional. By collecting relevant data and a list of questions or concerns you wish to address, you will be better prepared to keep the conference focused and positive.

91. **Parent contact should first begin when:**
(Average) (Skill 8.2)

    A.   You are informed the child will be your student

    B.   The student fails a test

    C.   The student exceeds others on a task

    D.   An IEP meeting is scheduled and you have had no previous replies to letters

Answer: A. You are informed the child will be your student
Student and parent contact should begin as a getting to know you piece, which allows you to begin on a non-judgmental platform. It is counterproductive to wait until there is a problem. If you can establish a cordial, team spirit relationship with the parents in the beginning, it will be easier to solve problems when they arise. It also helps the parent to see you as a professional that is willing to work with them.

92. **What can you do to create a good working environment with a classroom assistant?**
(Rigorous) (Skill 8.3)

    A.   Plan lessons with the assistant.

    B.   Write a contract that clearly defines his/her responsibilities in the classroom.

    C.   Remove previously given responsibilities.

    D.   All of the above

Answer: A. Plan lessons with the assistant
Planning with your classroom assistant shows that you respect his/her input and allows you to see where he/she feels confident.

93. **Which of the following describes the push-in teaching model?**
    (Easy) (Skill 8.3)

    A.   The general education teacher conducts the class while the special educator assists a student with disabilities one-on-one.

    B.   The special educator teaches parallel material in the general education classroom.

    C.   Both teachers actively teach in the general education classroom.

    D.   The general education teacher conducts the class after planning with the special educator how to differentiate activities to meet the needs of students with disabilities.

Answer: B. The special educator teaches parallel material in the general education classroom.
In the push-in teaching model, the special educator teaches parallel material in the general education classroom. The push-in teaching model is considered one type of differentiated instruction in which two teachers are teaching simultaneously.

94. **Janice requires occupational therapy and speech therapy services. She is your student. What must you do to ensure her needs are met?**
    (Rigorous) (Skill 8.4)

    A.   Watch the services being rendered.

    B.   Schedule collaboratively.

    C.   Ask for services to be given in a push-in model.

    D.   Ask them to train you to give the service.

Answer: B. Schedule collaboratively
Collaborative scheduling of students to receive services is both your responsibility and that of the service provider. Scheduling together allows for both your convenience and that of the service provider. It also will provide you with an opportunity to make sure the student does not miss important information.

95. **What can a teacher do to create a good working environment with a classroom assistant?**
(Rigorous) (Skill 8.4)

   A. Plan lessons with the assistant.

   B. Write a contract that clearly defines his or her responsibilities in the classroom.

   C. Remove previously given responsibilities.

   D. All of the above

Answer: A. Plan lessons with the assistant
Planning with a classroom assistant demonstrates that the teacher respects his or her input and allows the teacher to see where he or she feels confident.

96. **Which is a less-than-ideal example of collaboration in successful inclusion?**
(Rigorous) (Skill 8.4)

   A. Special education teachers are part of the instructional team in a regular classroom

   B. Special education teachers are informed of the lesson beforehand and assist regular education teachers in the classroom

   C. Teaming approaches are used for problem solving and program Implementation

   D. Regular teachers, special education teachers, and other specialists or support teachers co-teach

Answer: B. Special education teachers are informed of the lesson beforehand and assist regular education teachers in the classroom
In an inclusive classroom, all students need to see both teachers as equals. This situation places the special education teacher in the role of a paraprofessional/ teacher aide. Both teachers should be co-teaching in some way.

97. **A paraprofessional has been assigned to assist you in the classroom. What action on the part of the teacher would lead to a poor working relationship?**
(Average) (Skill 8.4)

   A.   Having the paraprofessional lead a small group

   B.   Telling the paraprofessional what you expect him/her to do

   C.   Defining classroom behavior management as your responsibility alone

   D.   Taking an active role in his/her evaluation

Answer: C. Defining classroom behavior management as your responsibility alone
When you do not allow another adult in the room to enforce the class rules, you create an environment where the other adult is seen as someone not to be respected. No one wants to be in a work environment where they do not feel respected.

98. **Mrs. Freud is a consultant teacher. She has two students with Mr. Ricardo. Mrs. Freud should:**
(Rigorous) (Skill 8.4)

   A.   Co-teach

   B.   Spend two days a week in the classroom helping out

   C.   Discuss lessons with the teacher and suggest modifications before class

   D.   Pull her students out for instructional modifications

Answer: C. Discuss lessons with the teacher and suggest modifications before class
Consultant teaching provides the least intervention possible for the success of the academic child. Pushing in or pulling out are not essential components. However, an occasional surveillance as a classroom observer who does not single out any students may also be helpful in providing modifications for the student.

99. **The most important member of the transition team is the** *(Easy) (Skill 8.5)*

     A.   Parent

     B.   Student

     C.   Secondary personnel

     D.   Postsecondary personnel

Answer: B. Student
Transition planning is a student-centered event that necessitates a collaborative endeavor. Responsibilities are shared by the student, parents, secondary personnel, and postsecondary personnel, who are all members of the transition team; however, it is important that the student play a key role in transition planning. This will entail asking the student to identify preferences and interests and to attend meetings on transition planning. The degree of success experienced by the student in postsecondary educational settings depends on the student's degree of motivation, independence, self-direction, self-advocacy, and academic abilities developed in high school. Student participation in transition activities should be implemented as early as possible and no later than age 16.

100. **If it is determined at a student's IEP meeting that some time in the general education setting is appropriate, which activities and/or classes** *might* **be included?**
     (Easy) (Skill 8.5)

     A.   Physical education

     B.   Math

     C.   Field trips

     D.   All of the above

Answer: D. All of the above
It may be determined at a student's IEP meeting that some time in the general education setting is appropriate. The activities and classes listed for inclusion may be field trips, lunch, recess, physical education, music, library, art, computers, math, science, social studies, spelling, reading, and/or English.